PROPHETIC MEDITATIONS ON ESTHER

Kingdom Keys To Save Our Nation

BY JOSEPHINE MARIE AYERS

xulon
PRESS

Table of Contents

Introduction vii
Dedications. ix
Endorsements. xiii
Forward xv

Meditation 1   Preparation 17
Meditation 2   Favor 20
Meditation 3   Obstacles and Trials. 23
Meditation 4   Authority and Favor 29
Meditation 5   More Tools for Effective
                       Intercession 33
Meditation 6   Birthing 38
Meditation 7   Exploits 40
Meditation 8   Signet Ring. 44
Meditation 9   Haman. 50
Meditation 10 Being at the right place at
                       the right time 57
Meditation 11 Oh my, what are we
                       going to do? 62
Meditation 12 Where is my miracle? Part 1 69
Meditation 13 Where is my miracle? Part 2 75
Meditation 14 Could you be a stealth for God? . . 84
Meditation 15 Feasts 89

Meditation 16 Healing practices to
                    facilitate healing. 96
Meditation 17 What is our response when
                    the King beckons? 102
Meditation 18 Joy comes in the morning 107
Meditation 19 Game changers for God 110
Meditation 20 Greater things: What is your
                    platform? 117
Meditation 21 The Journey. 123
Meditation 22 Disturbed. 129
Meditation 23 Me, an Oak! 135
Meditation 24 God's Tears 140
Meditation 25 Where the rubber hits the road! . 142
Meditation 26 Changed from the Inside Out!. . . 147

Epilogue-He is saving the best wine for last! . . . 157
References & footnotes 165
Author's Bio and contact. 169

Introduction

In March, 2014, I was led to start a closed group, a Facebook© (1) prayer page called Esther's Intercessors. In addition to having members post prayer and praise requests once a week on Friday, I started posting meditations, as well as words that God was downloading into me in relation to the Book of Esther, for whom the page was named. About two-thirds through the year, I began to feel that these "Friday Prophetic Meditations" would become a book-26 meditations in all.

I am keenly aware of current world situations and I can see that God is calling our generation up higher; to be Esthers, who will change our nation. But it starts inside of us. God is calling us up higher to pursue holiness and to fulfill our end-time destinies. I believe that these meditations (prophetic downloads) are 'Kingdom Keys'/strategies, sent by our LORD, for us to pursue towards the ends of Him healing our land. Remember in 2 Chronicles 7:14-15, *"...if My people who are called by My Name, shall humble themselves, and pray, and turn from their wicked ways; then I will hear from heaven, and will forgive their sin, and will heal their land. Now Mine eyes shall be open, and mine ears attentive, unto prayer that is made in this place."*

So, here we are, *"...for such a time as this"* (Esther 4:14d) and as Esther did, we must come before the King for the greater good.

I hope these meditations minister to the readers and inspire them to go up higher, to the plans and purposes God has for them, in this day, to do those greater things than these that Jesus did, and prophesied we would do in these Kingdom and end-times.

Living on the Edge of Glory,

Rev. Josephine M. Ayers

Dedications

First and foremost I want to thank the Lord Jesus for saving me and bringing me along in the most Holy Faith. He has been my friend, companion, confidant, inspiration, protection, and teacher, on this journey.

I also am grateful for a wonderful mother who always believed the best in me, and although in my younger days I did not understand it, I do now. She made me want to pursue excellence in all I do. One of her favorite sayings was, "Where there is a will, there is a way." He is my Way, (His Will is mine) my Truth and Life! Nothing is impossible with God! (When it was prophesied I would write a book, years ago, I laughed like Sarah did in Genesis 18:12.

I also want to thank ALL of my mentors along the way, and especially my sister in the Lord-Winnie Derning, and my spiritual mom-Kathy Orange, whose love, wisdom, prayers, encouragement, and wisdom are priceless to me. I also want to appreciative of all my awesome friends for their love and prayers. Thank you with all of my heart.

I want to thank my Spiritual Oversight in California -Glory Mountain International (2a), Mark and Deborah Griffo(2)- Sr. Pastors, for their continued prayers, love and belief in the Jesus in me, over many years. I also want to thank Pastors Brad and Carolyn Kuechler, (3) senior pastors of Rock Solid Revival Center (3a) Samaritan Walks (4) for their prophetic insight, prayers, and friendship, and Elim Gospel Church (5b) -Pastors Josh Finley (5) and Eric Scott,(5a) who have embraced the Jesus in me, and are my home away from home church family where I am currently serving.

I want to thank my husband David for supporting all that God is doing in my life.

I would also like to thank Karen Barnes, Lindie Lee Adamus, Kathy Davis , Billie Alexander, and Chris Kennedy for their input into this project and my life. I also want to thank last but not least, my life friend and sister-Debra Bendschneider. She was there for me when I needed the most love and support, and is still a rock solid influence in my life. I am blessed!

I am grateful for the Holy Spirit as He has been my ultimate teacher, mentor and guide, and given me purpose and strength and tenacity. Truly the anointing placed inside me has taught me along the way.

I thank God for being my 'Heavenly Poppa' for raising me from the dead, when I hit the ground in 2007. I look forward to completing my mission in life and finally, at the end, standing before Him and hopefully hearing, "Well done, good and faithful servant." He truly is the wind beneath my wings.

I am also thankful for my younger son Jeremy. Finally, thanks to my older son Christopher Hendrickson. He has been someone I admire, and a friend and peer, now that he is a man, husband and father!!! I learned how to love through being his mom, and it gives me great pleasure to see how he has matured and grown, and is continuing in his life, learning how to love. The most important role for me in this life has been that of mother. The way has not always been smooth, but the roots and love go deep, and the rewards many.

I am thankful for **all** the experiences in my life, and ALL the relationships that have molded me and continue to mold me into the person God wants me to be.

Josephine M. Ayers (Rev. Jo)
Jm.ayers@yahoo.com

Endorsements

Josephine Ayers has captured the heart of God for this season in which we live. Her book, "Prophetic Meditations on Esther, Kingdom Keys to Heal Our Land" will inspire, encourage and enlighten you to what God is doing right now. As you read you will not only develop a new hunger for God's presence, but you will gain rich prophetic insight into God's heart and mind. There are many great events happening in our world today that can easily distract us from what truly matters... time with God and hearing His voice. Thank you Josephine for your obedience in writing this insightful book and for your heart to help God's people discern the times in which we live and hear His voice for our everyday life.

–Pastor Brad Kuechler, M.A.–Founder and President of Samaritan's Walk International. Pastors for over 18 years Revivals to America
www.swalks.org

Prophetic Meditations on Esther is a powerful handbook written for this generation. If you are hungry for the presence of the Lord... read this book! It shows you how to touch the very heart of God.

Rene Picota(6), Lead Pastor, Streams of Life Church (6)a

I met Josephine on social media through my writings on 'Spirit Fuel'. As I read through her book, I was drawn in by her genuineness. It was as if we were having a conversation with each other. Each chapter was an easy read, and yet packed with powerful truths. It was insightful, challenging, and encouraging at the same time. She truly has an intercessors heart and a love for 'Poppa'. Be blessed!

Julie Price /Spirit Fuel Author (7)

Forward

Prophetic Meditations on Esther is a book written with declarations for, *'Such a time as this'*. (Esther 4:14b) The word-*declare* means to: make known formally or officially, to proclaim, to state authoritatively or affirm. Josephine Ayers makes several GOD breathed declarations that will empower your life for destiny. It will awaken your spiritual senses to all that God has for you. It will literally assist you in bringing Heaven on earth in your daily living.

The Book of Esther reveals the true beauty of our Savior. It encourages us to have no compromise in our Christian walk. It speaks to us in our walk with the LORD, and helps us to become aware to the times and seasons of our life. It demonstrates honor. It reveals the secrets of sowing and reaping, and what it means to be a son or daughter of the King. It proclaims a resounding victory for impact in society, and all that God has called us as believers.

As you read through this book you will see favor with authority. It reveals the heart of effective intercession and it allows you to be awakened to miracles and healing. It provides tools to overcome trials. It will also help you to declare on a daily basis the principals and power of GOD for your life.

It is with great joy that I encourage you to read this book. Read it word for word, and hear the explicit truth that will literally change your life. Let it bring explosive revelation, assisting you every day in victorious Christian living!

In addition, this book will help you see the impact of one's life upon a nation in history. God has called each and every one of us to bring change and become history makers. May as you as the reader become inspired to bring an atmosphere of heaven to each and every situation you face in life.

My prayer for you as you read this book is, "May you will daily rest from your enemies. May God turn each month of your life into gladness. May God take you from mourning in to delight. May God give to you days of feasting and gladness. May the Lord give abundance so that you will pour life and gifts into others."

This book is one of those gifts.
Pastor Mark A. Griffo
Glory Mountain
www.glorymountain.com

MEDITATION 1

Preparation

In her lifetime, Esther had a powerful impact on the Jewish Nation. Before she was presented to the king, and subsequently chosen queen, Esther submitted herself to a twelve month beauty regime that not only included the use oil of myrrh, perfumes and cosmetics, but she was also given special foods and privileges. She may have been taught the protocols of court. (Esther 2:9, 12-14)

While we believers in the natural are not required to use exotic treatments or perfumes before being presented to King Jesus; God in His Grace, has clothed us with the anointing and empowerment of the Holy Spirit, and given us the Bible to instruct and guide us through this life. What He requires of us is: obedience, holiness, humility, and prayer. Once prepared, then we are launched into our destiny in Him.

In Esther's story, a royal decree was issued to kill of all the Jews. Following this news, the Jews of the empire united in prayer for deliverance. The New Testament confirms, *"...The prayer of a righteous person is powerful and effective.* (James 5:16) Esther joined too, and was impressed by God to prepare to go unsummoned before the King to plead for her people. Her Uncle Mordecai, prophetically (a type of the Holy Spirit), sent word to her, *"Yet who knows if you have been called here for such a time as this!"* (Esther 4:14)

This action would be perilous for Esther because it was against the law to appear before the king unsummoned; but I believe God, Who is sovereign, was directing, orchestrating and responding to the people's prayers. We see later that His protection was with her during her encounter with the King. (Hebrews 4:16 tells us that we can approach His throne with confidence and grace.)

While the people continued to pray, the Holy Spirit led Esther to undertake a special fast, what some call a *'Breakthrough Fast'*. In v16 of that same chapter, she orders her handmaidens and friends to a 3-day fast with no food or water. (We must remember that we cannot manipulate the Hand of God by making random decisions based on what people before us may have done. Just because it worked for Esther here, does not mean that is exactly what we should do in a different situation. We need to know in any given situation exactly what God wants us to do.)

In the same way as Esther, we also need to learn our destinies and anointing's and then aggressively move in them as she did. We don't want to miss God's opportunities!

Much is said about fasting and prayer in scripture. Let's go to Isaiah 58, which is often called the fasting chapter. In this case, it was prophetic direction from God specifically to the hypocritical religious leaders, who paraded themselves in their good deeds and 'fasting' efforts, but missed the heart of God. What the Lord said to them in verse 6 is, *"Is not this the kind of fasting I have chosen: to loose the chains of injustice and untie the cords of the yoke, to set the oppressed free and break every yoke?"*

Here, what I see is God pointing out is that there is a higher fast, and it is not just food and drink! Let's ask God this week the direction He would have us go in our intercessory prayer life. Does it include fasting? We should not fast without direction from God, and for those with physical challenges, without guidance from physicians.

But when He is in it, (whatever the type of fast He is calling us to) and we are to be obedient. When we employ faith and obedience, we can watch the mountains move. In accord with His directions, we will have His Ear as well as His Will!!!

MEDITATION 2

Favor

The Book of Esther is about many things, one of which is *favor*. Queen Esther received great favor in the sight of the King. I see some interesting Biblical principles operating with regard to favor in the Book of Esther.

Webster's Dictionary (8) defines *favor in* several ways, some of which are: good will; kindness; a kind act; a token of good; advantage, to show partiality to; to facilitate. How many of these do you see in the Book of Esther?

Esther's faith *transcended* circumstances that could have destroyed her life, and it operated as child-like faith as she submitted herself to Mordecai's wisdom and persuading.

Matthew 6:33 says, *"... But seek first his kingdom and his righteousness, and all these things will be given to you..."* It is clear Esther had a "kingdom" mentality and put God first, despite her circumstances.

"For the eyes of the LORD range throughout the earth to strengthen those whose hearts are fully committed to him." (2 Chronicles 16:9) Esther was one who was fully committed to Him, so He protected her.

"When the LORD takes pleasure in anyone's way, He causes their enemies to make peace

with them."(Proverbs 16:7) Because God was pleased with Esther, He protected her so she could safely invite the enemy to eat with her at the Kings table!

Hebrews 11:39 states how the elders received a good report. Abraham's belief in God's Word to him was what was accounted to him as righteousness. He believed and obeyed God when it made no sense to him: *Abraham laid his son on an altar to kill him,* but the Lord intervened because God was proving him to see what kind of stuff Abraham was made of and if he would obey, as hard as this command was. (Genesis 22:9)

I can say first-hand that the Lord has had me do some *'out of the box'* stuff, but it always bore fruit! Those of you who know my testimony can bear witness to this. But again, He is an out of the box God, Who, from what I read, likes to *'stir the pot'!*

God wanted to prove Esther, to see if she would lay down her fear for her life and for her nation. Would she have *faith* to *obey?* Obedience brings great favor!

Esther was humble as well, kneeling quietly before the throne. Humility, too, brings great favor! And the King ended up extending his scepter to her and offering to her up to half the kingdom.

We can see how Esther modeled these principles, and the fruit was the tremendous favor with the King: she and her people were saved, and the enemy destroyed.

So let us ponder this: in what ways can we follow these principles of Faith and Obedience and so position ourselves to receive increased favor from our King?

Let's pray:

Lord, we love and praise You. We thank You for the favor You have given us, and we pray that we would receive the promise of Ephesians 3:20, *"Now to Him who is able to do exceedingly abundantly (immeasurably, as one version states) above all that we ask or think, according to the power that works in us"*... Favor like we have never experienced before, for your Glory; and empowering for the call You place on us in this day and in these times!

We thank you in Jesus Name. Amen.

MEDITATION 3

Obstacles and Trials

The Lord has had me thinking about obstacles and trials in our lives. How do we view them?

Do we see them as stepping stones along the way to becoming perfected in Christ; or as opportunities for God to reveal His Glory in us and in our testimonies? (Please note the word testimony starts with test.) You can't have a testimony without a test!

Or, do we see obstacles and trials as God's anger or rejection? Are we mad at, or ashamed of ourselves? (I know first-hand that a spirit of unworthiness can really hinder belief for the supernatural in our prayers or in our daily walk). Young Christians in the Lord often err and equate the person of God, with the model of their earthly dads-ordinary mortals, who may have had some issues or failings. We must guard ourselves and correct our perspective on God to what is taught of His real nature in the Scriptures so we don't fall into these pits.

A few years ago I had the privilege of ministering in a women's prison. At that time the Lord impressed on me that these women were struggling. They did not believe that God would answer their prayers because of their unworthiness- their sin (those actions that got them

23

there). Such thoughts consumed them! When I ministered about this, God met them and many were delivered into a new freedom with God! Many began having answered prayers. Why? They now were praying as daughters and sons of a King, not prisoners loaded down with guilt and shame.

I woke up this morning with two scriptures: Psalm 40:2, *"He lifted me out of the slimy pit, out of the mud and mire; He set my feet on a rock and gave me a firm place to stand."* 1 Peter 5:10, *"And the God of all grace, who called you to His eternal glory in Christ, after you have suffered a little while, will make Himself to restore you and make you strong, firm and steadfast..."*

The Bible does not equate prosperity or lack of trials, with righteousness or how much faith we have, or how much favor we have with God. Our circumstances do not dictate or dominate who we are in Christ! We must learn to stand on that!

The Bible talks about hard stuff: suffering and what that produces. When we first come to Christ and offer ourselves to be used by Him, we have no clue what that could mean! Look at the lives of the martyrs. I would say they are special to Jesus, His word says so, but hardly what I would call an abundant life. We need to remember that our Hope is above: He is with us, He will lift us, He will strengthen us, and He will make us strong, firm, and steadfast.

Other scriptures show that suffering produces the fruits of perseverance, faith, and character. We need to see that obstacles are ladder rungs of opportunity to a higher ground with Christ. There is a fellowship born of intimacy with Christ in our sufferings that cannot be denied, but no one wants to talk about it.

The Bible also says the servant is not greater than the Master. As He was not excused from suffering, His followers may have to face it, too. I also think some folks miss the eternal perspective of being prepared for Glory. We get involved with living and surviving and miss the Creator's perspective. Instead, our ears tune in to things called abundant life. But if we are not riding high economically, we are made to feel like failures, because the world has determined the definition of *'abundant'*.

Esther had a destiny. She came from a humble Jewish family and was faced with a difficult process of being prepared to meet her King. She embraced it all, and not once she did complain, or fear, even though she did not know the outcome. She poised herself, focused on her God, and moved ahead.

King David focused on God when facing the giant. He used his sling and some stones to kill him. In the Bible, stones represent many things. One "stone" he hurled was a carefully placed prayer (carried by the Angel of the Lord to just the right spot on that giant's forehead, and wham!

We need to guard our thought life and keep the correct perspective about obstacles and trials: <u>they are stepping stones to God's purposes!</u>

We need to have a mind focused on Christ and know His nature. If we know what He is about, we would always know that He has our best in mind, no matter what it takes to get there. His will always prevails.

We need to keep our focus and not allow distractions or hindrances to slow us down. Delay does not mean denial, however, we must keep in mind God is Sovereign and He gets to call the shots. When we don't get the answer we want when we pray, we need to consider His timing and also ask, is it in line with His will for us?

I have heard so many times, Isaiah 53:5, *"But he was pierced by our transgressions, he was crushed for our iniquities, the punishment that brought us peace was on him, and by his wounds we are healed."* Yes, that refers to our spiritual healing and reconciliation with the Father. He does allow things in our lives that we may or may not understand. Will we be yielding, like Job, and say, *"Though He slay me, yet will I hope in him...*" (Job 13:15) God allowed Job many afflictions. The Bible also says, "*The righteous person may have many troubles, but the Lord delivers him out of all of them...*" (Psalms 34:19)

Often, we just don't know what His deliverance looks like. We may be looking in the wrong direction. Does He allow Christians to suffer and be martyred and persecuted? God always has the higher good in mind and my mind usually cannot encompass the hugeness of our God. Truly, His ways are far too marvelous and wondrous to me!

Remember these principles:

- Know who we are in Christ, and the authority He gives us. (Condemnation is not from God).

- Keep our hearts pure and our hands clean.

- Persevere in our prayers, even when we hit speed bumps and pot holes and it *feels* like the prayers must be falling on deaf ears (this is where Satan really can play with your head). Don't give up.

Let's use the weapon God has given us: *prayer.* Aim prayers led by the Spirit, and shoot! If the weapon is not picked up and the trigger not pulled, the ammo won't connect with the target!

The best weapon I see is praise and thanks. As with the popular song that led Jehoshaphat's army in 2 Chronicles 20:21b says:

> *"...Give thanks to the Lord, for his love endures forever. "*

MEDITATION 4

Authority and Favor

What are we doing with the authority and favor that God has given us?

You say, 'What authority'?

All through scripture there are numerous references to God giving us authority! It started right at the beginning in Genesis 1:26, when we are given dominion over the Earth. That's authority over everything, from the animals and plants, to treading on snakes and scorpions and the demonic, in Jesus' Name. Then, the Lord Jesus cranked it up and said to His disciples that *we (paraphrased) would do greater things than He did, in this age and time* (John 14:12). So, what are we doing with this knowledge?

> In 2 Timothy 3:5 the verse speaks of people *"having a form of godliness, but denying its power. Have nothing to do with such people."*

God also gave us the authority to decree! Look at Job 22:28,

> *"You will also declare a thing, And it will be established for you; So light will shine on your ways."* (NKJV)

29

Is there something that needs to happen in your life, just waiting for you to speak it into being? This verse shows us that when we have faith to declare God's will, He will establish it, and light will come to us. So, here's the pattern: I believe God, I say it, and God agrees with it, it is done!

Proverbs 18:21 says, *"The tongue has the power of life and death..."* How do you use your tongue? How much do your words weigh? What do you speak on a daily basis? Is it a seemingly innocent cliché? Your speech and use of your tongue can produce events or changes in our lives. For instance, we can curse ourselves, saying such things as, "I'm stupid, or you are stupid." Maybe you say, "Oh, that ____ is killing me." Have you ever said that before? Another is, "I am sorry," over and over, and so we become a sorry person. There are many others: "I am mad", or "I am sad", "What do I know?" These are decrees that will have a negative effect and cause us to become what we say.

We need to learn God's assignments for us, our identities in Him, and our God- given authority, and decree (speak) in harmony with those! We have the power to bind and loose, or pronounce life or death! I believe there is so much we are missing out on because we are not utilizing the empowerments we have been given in Him. From what I see in the Word, I believe that we have the power to change our circumstances and our environments for Him.

In Joshua 10:12-13, *"On the day the LORD gave the Amorites over to Israel, Joshua said to the LORD in the presence of Israel: Sun, stand still over Gibeon, and you, moon, over the Valley of Aijalon." So the sun stood still, and the moon stopped, till the nation avenged itself on its enemies..."* And it did! Joshua needed time for the battle and put God on the spot to do something huge!

Then there was Elijah, who called forth fire during his encounter with the prophets of Baal! (1 Kings 18:38)

What secret did these men have? They were not using their own strength; they were praying and decreeing with the authority given to them through God, who establishes everything.

There is a difference between prophecy and decreeing. Prophecy is a foretelling of what is on God's heart; decreeing, on the other hand is an establishing of an event or thing God has prompted someone to do. The Holy Spirit broods over us to assemble our words according to His heart, and then prompts us to speak forth 'Truth and Light 'so as to have it established. I believe we have a holy obligation to use our tongues wisely.

Let's move on to favor! Esther had favor and authority and she used both to change her environment, as in Esther 9:29, when she wrote with all authority to confirm the second letter of Purim. Do we act similarly?

Favor is better than silver or gold. The latter are fleeting, power is fleeting, too; but favor is everlasting and eternal, and encompasses all we are and do! Do we have favor we have not yet exercised, and are we prepared to use it for His Kingdom Glory? Think about this

We decree and God establishes. We use our favor to change our environment for God! It is not all about what it can do for us, as much as what we can do for God! We are His mouthpieces here on Earth.

We are here for such a time as this! Let's make the most of it.

MEDITATION 5

More Tools for Effective Intercession

Two weeks ago I started having flashes in my right eye. Almost immediately the Lord spoke to my spirit and I heard something like, *'He would help me see better'*. In my mind, I wondered, physically or spiritually?

As time progressed my vision became blurry and new floaters appeared; and I had three eye doctors' visits. I learned I had a benign retinal detachment, with similar symptoms to a retinal detachment. I learned this would NEVER again be a concern for this particular eye. I had survived the worst.

A couple of nights ago I was rubbing my eyes and inadvertently a foreign body lodged itself in my right eye. It felt like a 'boulder' was in there! I poured copious amounts of sterile saline in it, looked, and looked some more, applied some eye salve, but all to no avail! I was happy it was bed time and I would not have to endure the discomfort.

Before I closed my eyes I said to the Lord, I am not sure why this is happening, but somehow You will work it to good; please give me the grace to withstand the terrible discomfort and to discern what it is You are trying to show me.

I awoke the next morning to the same condition as the night before. Almost immediately I thought that the increase in sight was going to be some spiritual nugget! Well, as the morning progressed I reluctantly called the eye doctor and scheduled another appointment for that afternoon. At that point I thought I might even have scratched my cornea!

During all this, there was another matter pressing heavily on my heart and as I prepared for the day I was overcome in my emotions and began to sob and sob. I stuck my face in a towel and, as my daughter-in-law put it later, I literally cried out to God.

When I pulled my face out of the towel I suddenly realized the pain and 'boulder' were gone. The very thing that made me cry became the vehicle to my deliverance! I began to praise and thank God for the very things that made me cry!

In this experience, He has shown me a few things:

- My crying, I believe, was perceived by God as intercession, and as my Godly daughter-in-law, told me, He healed me! There was so much passion behind the tears. Often there are situations in our lives that leave us literally speechless, but as our spirits cry out to God, tears begin to flow. Don't discount tears! They are not a sign of weakness; tears can move mountains, as well as God's heart.

- God is a God of sudden-lies, and we need to expect to have them.

- He is a big-picture God; even when we don't ask, He is busy planning our deliverance. Truly, *"...all things work together for good..."* (Romans 8:28), and we must not despise those things that afflict us; maybe, just maybe, these are our vehicles to deliverance, like what happened in my case. There is a spirit that says, 'a righteous Christian is affliction-less'. But the Bible says, *"The righteous cry out, and the Lord hears them; he delivers them from all their troubles."* (Psalm 34:19)

- I did not complain, I just praised Him. In fact, I kept uttering the prayer over and over in 1 Chronicles 16:34, *"Give thanks to the Lord, for he is good; his love endures forever."*

- I also asked Him for grace to deal with all of my other sorrow, and told Him I was trusting that He would intervene, somehow! I trusted He had my good at heart, but I was miserable and uncomfortable with this issue with my eye.

Tears are cleansing, literally in my case! They are a vehicle to spiritual and emotional release. I believe tears are often the first line of intercession. I dug into Esther a little further. In Esther 4:1b & 3, the first thing Mordecai did when he heard of the plot to kill the Jews was to cry. It reads, *"...He let out a loud and bitter cry... in every province where the King's command and decree arrived, there was great mourning among the Jews, with fasting, weeping and wailing; and many lay in sackcloth and ashes."* In John 11:35, (regarding Lazarus' death), *"Jesus wept."* In the Garden of Gethsemane, Jesus also wept so profoundly his tears turned to blood!

Weeping and wailing create a passionate and explosive synergy that propels effective and powerful intercession! I believe hard times are used by God to catapult us into a place of greater vision and revelation. They even are the vehicle for our deliverance, if we let them be; and also look for it and expect it, and decree it, so He may establish it!

"Let Me help you see as I do," says the Lord, in one of Marsha and Bill Burns, Small *Straws in a Soft Wind (9), daily online prophetic words.*

I am amazed at how God uses profound circumstances and on multiple levels to achieve His purposes. For instance, consider the path that God made for the children of Israel through the Red Sea. It also became the path for Pharaoh's final demise! God does not waste a thing.

"For His anger is but for a moment, but his favor lasts a lifetime; weeping may remain for a night, but rejoicing comes in the morning." (Psalm 30:5) Sometimes, morning does tarry, but it does come!

MEDITATION 6

Birthing

The Lord began speaking to me about 'birthing' today. I feel He has impressed on me there are many 'births' about to come forth! That is, it feels as though the 'pregnancy,' 'process has been going on, the 'waters' have broken, and delivery has begun. Labor is starting out slow, but has been progressing; ('transition') the worst part of the labor, is now upon the body of Christ! It feels awful! Pains are coming every two minutes, and without reprieve; the 'body 'feels nauseated. Thinking is also confused, often not rational, but we are on track for a wonderful birth!

During the transition there is questioning and even thinking you would never do it again, or it is someone's fault, and all you can think about is getting this baby out! There are many midwives to attend this birth who have been faithfully and watchfully interceding and praising God to facilitate it. I hear *'push, push, push through the pain, it will all be worth it'*. Romans 8:26-28 (The Message) says, *"Meanwhile, the moment we get tired in the waiting, God's Spirit is right alongside helping us along. If we don't know how or what to pray, it doesn't matter. He does our praying in and for us, making prayer out of our wordless sighs, our aching groans. He knows us far better than we know ourselves, knows our pregnant condition, and keeps us present before God. That's why we can be so sure that every detail in our lives of love for God is worked into something good."*

Then, Isaiah42:9 came to me: *"See, the former things have taken place, and new things I declare; before they spring into being I announce them to you."* (By the way, this word is not just for women, it is for men as well, and who have been laboring in prayer!)

I think about all Esther went through for that Kairos moment with the King, when an entire Kingdom was transformed forever! I think of how she was anointed queen and all that led up to opened doors and precedents for a new order in the Kingdom of Susa: a Divine Order there that never existed.

A new order is coming folks!

We are only given a small glimpse into Esther's life, but you can bet she was a 'forerunner' in this land, and that the combination of her queen-ship, her favor, her authority, the King, and Mordecai's help removed bondages, broke chains, released new anointing, and changed lives forever. She was a mountain shaker and a world changer in that day.

MEDITATION 7

Exploits

Have you prepared for great exploits? Are you praying God's heart and his vision on a matter? God equipped Esther for the task at hand and for the vision she was to have, even before she knew it!

"Where there is no vision, the people perish: But he that keepeth the law, happy is he." (*Prov.* 29:18 KJV) The Hebrew word for vision here is *prophetic revelation;* we can further define it as divine illumination, God's heart on the matter!

I really like how this same passage is worded in The Message: *"If people can't see what God is doing, they stumble all over themselves; But when they attend to what he reveals, they are much blessed."*

Here is the formula: Proper information + Spiritual illumination = Vision.

Vision brings motivation and protection! Esther got the vision.

I see several steps in this process. In Esther Chapter 2, Esther was an orphan. Mordecai, her uncle (a type of the Holy Spirit) adopted and raised her; (the work of salvation is done by the Holy Spirit) when she was adopted by him, her whole life changed.

Romans 8:15 (NKJV) says, *"For you did not receive the spirit of bondage again to fear, but you received the Spirit of adoption, by whom we call out "Abba, Father."* Holy Spirit is God and Esther called Mordecai-Poppa.

This is how I see the prophetic progression in Esther 2:

1- Esther became aware of her identity in Him. In v7 she was chosen and adopted by Mordecai and submitted herself to his wisdom and authority.

2- In v12 she was prepared and purified for her moment with the King. She submitted to six months' of anointing oils (empowerment), six months of perfumes (the aroma of the Lord surrounding her, which is His presence).

3- In v19 she was given the vision by Mordecai (informed of the plan, God's heart on the matter + proper information=vision).

4- Mordecai cried out, along with the nation, and there was a call to prayer and fasting (we have already covered this).

5- Esther saw the opportunity (Kairos moment) and acted. The rest is history: she went on to save a nation.

So, we have a recipe, if you will, for praying on target, for acting with preciseness and deliberateness in order to bring about His will for a specific time: always ready, instant in and out of season, prophetic intercession and action at its best!

In the late 1990's we went to a prophetic conference in Colorado Springs. A man from England was there and gave this testimony. He was working in a factory and there was an alarm for a bomb scare. All were told to evacuate the building and go into the streets. The Holy Spirit prompted him to go into the cafeteria. This Divine revelation was so strong he did not ignore it and went to the cafeteria, as nonsensical as this seemed; *the bomb went off in the street.*

God gives His people the tools they need in all times. Esther spent so much time in His presence, and was so humble and submitted when the vision came there was no static on her line; she was clean and clear to receive it! His Presence in her life made for her favor, vision, motivation, empowerment, and protection, effective in both intercession and victory.

This is what He has for us today as His children! He is the same God that saves. He is the same cloud that shielded the children of Israel from their enemies and the heat of the desert, and the light that guided them across the Red Sea!

Thank you, Lord, for providing us all we need to navigate through life; may we always be sensitive to Your voice and bidding, and the vision, for it is Your vision for our lives!

Here's a quote from Prophet Bill Yount (10): *"Peter sank, but he walked on water. Sinking is better than sitting. When life is over we won't regret taking a risk for God and sinking. We will regret sitting. And God won't remember us sinking,"*

MEDITATION 8

Signet Ring

The Lord has been speaking to me about 'being made a signet ring,' as in His conversation with Zerubbabel in Haggai chapter 2:23. What is a signet ring?

In the ancient world and up into modern times, a ruler's signet ring constituted an official seal, which when used, meant that a document was official, or that a letter or package could not be opened except by the addressee. Whoever owned the ring had the power.

In Strong's Concordance of the Bible (11)-#2885 *tabba`athtab-bah'-ath* (from 2883) it says, "a seal (as sunk into the wax), i.e. signet (for sealing); hence (generally) a ring of any kind."

Not only in the Book of Esther, which we have been studying, but in several other places in the Bible, there are references to rings and signet rings. The first is in Genesis 41:42: *"Then Pharaoh took off his ring from his finger and put it upon Joseph's finger. He dressed him in robes of fine linen, and put a gold chain about his neck."*

Another is in Haggai 2:20-23 (NKJV), concerning Zerubbabel, 'the Lord's Signet Ring.' *"And again the word of the LORD came to Haggai*

*on the twenty-fourth day of the month, saying,
"Speak to Zerubbabel, governor of Judah, saying:*

'I will shake heaven and earth.

I will overthrow the throne of kingdoms;

*I will destroy the strength of the Gentile
kingdoms.*

I will overthrow the chariots

And those who ride in them;

The horses and their riders shall come down,

Everyone by the sword of his brother.

*'In that day,' says the LORD of hosts, 'I will
take you, Zerubbabel My servant, the son of
Shealtiel,' says the LORD, 'and will make you
like a signet ring; for I have chosen you,' says
the LORD of hosts."*

Zerubbabel, the governor in Judah under
King Darius, had been one of three of King
Darius' guards. His debating skills won him
great favor with that king. He is also credited
as the one used by God to re-establish the
Davidic dynasty in Israel and the return of
Judah (praise) to Israel.

The signet reference in Esther is found in
Esther 8:2. *"And the king took off his signet
ring, which he had taken from Haman, and
gave it unto Mordecai; and Esther appointed
Mordecai over the house of Haman."*

The signet ring in scripture holds great significance. As in the natural realm, so it is in the spiritual realm: the signet ring represents authority and permanence of that authority; it represents restoration and redemption, favor, and God's protection. And it can also represent judgement.

In Esther 8, King Ahasuerus had given Haman the rank of grand vizier, and with that rank, the king's signet ring. This occurred prior to the king's having knowledge of Haman's plot to eradicate all the Jews. It is noteworthy that later, when the king removed his ring from the hand of Haman, Haman was speedily sentenced to death by being hanged on the gallows.

This is of great significance because further along in Esther we read that there is a transfer of power along with the signet ring...like with the anointing of the Holy Spirit. Notice, when King Ahasuerus gave Mordecai (the servant) the ring by placing it on his hand, Esther in turn gave Mordecai (the servant) the house/palace of Haman. Total reversal!

Indeed, as Esther further pursued her case with the king, he delegated additional authority. It is written in Esther 8:8,10(KJV), *"Write ye also for the Jews, as it liketh you, in the king's name, and seal it with the king's ring: for the writing which is written in the king's name, and sealed with the king's ring, may no man reverse...10 And he wrote in King Ahasuerus' name, and sealed it with the king's ring, and sent letters by posts on horseback, and riders on mules, camels, and young dromedaries..."*

Sealed, in Strong's, # 2856: chatham khawtham, a primitive root; to close up; especially to seal, make an end, mark, seal (up), stop.

The last Bible reference that I will refer to for my purposes is Luke 15:22(ESV), *"But the father said to his servants, Bring quickly the best robe, and put it on him, and put a ring on his hand, and shoes on his feet."*

Not only did rulers have signets, but so did heads of families and households, as did the father in this verse from the story of the return of the prodigal son. The ring restored the son to his position of authority.

In Western culture we have inherited the sense of the signet in the marital relationship. When a man proposes marriage to his sweetheart and she responds by saying yes, he places a ring on her hand. She now belongs solely unto him as his betrothed wife. She will bear his name and his legal children, and have authority to carry out his will by representing him in all matters while he is off providing income for the family.

God uses a signet ring to mark His chosen. The elect of God have the seal of the Holy Spirit of promise (Ephesians 1:13) upon their fore-heads. They are identifiable in the spiritual realm and always have a desire in their heart and mind to do the will of God, their Lord. Along with sealing comes favor, as God extends his scepter to us. When we come before Him in prayer with our petitions, we can expect to see answers unfold before our eyes.

Receiving the seal of God's signet ring, His impress on us, is a permanent, non-reversible occurrence! We now possess, by the power of the Holy Spirit, the authority to move forward, to be used as instruments to make permanent changes in this age. We need to understand this and realize our potential in prophetic intercession.

I don't believe these principles are limited to the Biblical times I referenced. Today, we need be aware of the signet rings given us by God and move and walk in the authority He has given us. Joseph, Esther and Zerubbabel were instrumental in saving a nation because of their rings.

Second Chronicles 7:14 says, *"...if my people, who are called by name, will humble themselves and pray and seek my face and turn from their wicked ways, then I will hear from heaven, and I will forgive their sin and heal their land."*

If we want to see this nation change, WE must change and seek His face. We can debate and complain all we want about what is swirling around us, but God's direction is clear. When we do our part, He will do His! When our prayer work is done, stamped, signed, sealed, and delivered, God will see that it will be established!

It is a great privilege to be equipped by God to be used in this way: His signet rings.

MEDITATION 9

Haman

The Lord began inspiring me about Haman, the villain in the book of Esther. So I thought,' who wants to give him any due'?

But the Lord began to impress on me that there are lessons to be learned from the Haman's mistakes. These mistakes led to his demise. So, yes, let's take a closer look at this man known as 'The Enemy of the Jews'.

A good title for this chapter would be-Knowing Your Enemy When You Go into Battle. From a military standpoint, there always has to be a plan and a strategy for battle. The army is delegated authority from the commander-in-chef to overcome and annihilate the enemy. The ranks of the military are under the authority of the top officers, who guide and direct them in the best plan available for the task.

Before every plan is developed in the military, much time is given to learning about the enemy: their location, their strengths, their habits, and their vulnerabilities. This information is matched up with our own strengths and weaknesses, which then must be corrected. That process is called- acquiring intelligence.

In matters of spiritual warfare, to acquire intelligence, it is necessary that we enter into prophetic intercession, and the Holy Spirit, Who is with us, will reveal to us how to pray effectively, on target, and with authority against our spiritual enemy. If we are honest and willing, He also will reveal to us our own vulnerabilities.

> (Jesus said), *"I have given you authority to trample on snakes and scorpions and to overcome all the power of the enemy; nothing will harm you."* (*Luke* 10:19)

First, we must know our new identity in Christ in order to accomplish this. (I cannot emphasize this enough!) Secondly, we must learn if there are residual things in our own souls that might hinder us in this process?

While I was preparing to minister in a women's prison in California, the Lord showed me I had some spiritual baggage in the way. I'm often perplexed why I can believe for someone else for something, and it would happen, but not for myself. It was frustrating. I consider myself a person of faith, but something was in the way...the Lord was right!

The Holy Spirit quickly opened my eyes and ears to the presence of a spirit of unworthiness that I still had league with! So, that was what was standing in the way of believing that God loved me enough to answer my prayers in

PROPHETIC MEDITATIONS ON ESTHER

spite of the slime of the past and of my being let down by others.

Another hindrance was that I really was not knowledgeable enough about God's nature and ways to recognize when lies about Him were spoken to me. This was, and is, a powerful strategy of the enemy!

We must realize that we are in a war! There are spiritual strategies against us to make us limp and ineffective Christians, impotent before the enemy. One of the biggest is lies about God. We need to examine any and all things that we believe about God to see if they are lies. If you are unsure, ask a person who knows God well. When you know the truth, it is easy to discern the lies.

The next step is to deal with it, and so I did! God in His infinite mercy began to reveal Himself and His Person to me to further dismantle a host of lies I believed. All these had been hindering me to becoming all that I could be as a person and a minister.

I took this message to the women in prison. It was amazing what happened that night. Now mind you, these women were in prison, so reminders of their sins were all around them.

The first thing they needed to do was to forgive themselves. The Lord tells us to forgive, or we won't be forgiven. That includes us/

ourselves. Once they did that, then they asked God's forgiveness.

Second, we need to get rid of unbelief which dams up the flow of God's blessing. The women were able to renounce this and move into receiving instead.

Third, we should know God's love and His truth. When the women understood this, there came a newly found faith that God had something good for them. They began to realize that they were joint heirs with Christ, and could really understand the price He paid for them

Fourth, I began to show them the power of binding and loosing, according to scripture: *"Truly I tell you, whatever you bind on earth will be bound in heaven, and whatever you loose on earth will be loosed in heaven."* (Matthew 18:18)

During the ministry time you could see them opening up like flowers, and even their prayers were bolder and with more authority. The scheme of the enemy had been exposed, and over time we began to hear testimonies of answered prayers!

By illustration, during a recent phone call with someone experiencing a trial, that person brought to my attention a 'deceitful and lying' spirit!

The Holy Spirit brought back to my mind about our ability to bind and loose the Spirit. I was given a better strategy to pray more effectively for this particular battle; and I got busy. I asked the Lord to help me discern the evil spirits operating here so we could take care of business.

Let us go back to Haman.

Haman's first mistake was his pride! *"When Haman saw that Mordecai would not kneel down or pay him honor, he was enraged."* (Esther 3:5)

Second, pride opened the door and invited in spirits of betrayal, greed, control, manipulation, and conspiracy. *"Then Haman said to King Xerxes, There is a certain people dispersed among the peoples in all the provinces of your kingdom who keep themselves separate. Their customs are different from those of all other people, and they do not obey the king's laws; it is not in the king's best interest to tolerate them."* (Esther 3:8) Each one of those spirits was operating in Haman. He convinced the king that all of the Jews needed to be eliminated.

Through Mordecai, the Holy Spirit gave the strategy to undo the mess. Esther had been prepared, she obeyed, and the nation was saved. She knew who she was, what her authority was, and she used it.

We need to be like Esther in a world of full of Hamans. We need to pray and ask God if unworthiness is a hindrance in our prayer lives, and if so, allow Him to remove it from us. We need to move assertively into a place of being powerful prophetic intercessors on matters (knowing the heart of God), rather than settling for Godliness without power, as Scripture says.

We are not slaves to our past, our circumstances, or what others have imposed on us. We are new creations (creatures) in Christ. We need to take up the swords He has given us (the Word of God and Divine revelation); then we can take back our land and our circumstances; and from our position of being seated with Him in heavenly places, move into victory.

That is what God has for us; anything else is a lie.

It's easy to lose sight of some of these tools because of circumstances closing in, from personal defeats, or from lack of use. Scripture says we are to keep alert, so let's wake up and be ready at all times.

I feel strongly, as we come into this next move of God, it is going to be the raising up an army of *prophetic* evangelists. We will be loosed in the marketplace and begin to pray for people prophetically. They will surrender into repentance, healing, and with signs and wonders following. As Esther's time of preparation concluded and her time of destiny began, our time of preparation is ending, and I believe the time is at hand for the biggest move of God ever. And we have a part in it.

Let's make sure we are ready for such a time as this. It is time for a period of self-examination and inventory, to see if there are any chinks in our spiritual armor. Times are complex; the battle's raging hotter; but the empowerment from the Lord will meet those challenges. Are we ready for the strategy of the battles?

We who have been in ministry awhile cannot fall into spiritual complacency, thinking we are on top of it.

> "*Be alert and of sober mind. Your enemy the devil prowls around like a roaring lion looking for someone to devour.*" (1 Peter 5:8)

But, be of good cheer: "*For the eyes of the Lord range throughout the earth to strengthen those whose hearts are fully committed to him...*" (2 Chronicles 16:9a)

Therefore, "*You, dear children, are from God and have overcome them, because the one who is in you is greater than the one who is in the world.*" (1 John 4:4)

Let us not forget to whom we belong!

MEDITATION 10

Being at the Right Place at the Right Time

In Esther 4:14b Mordecai speaks to Esther and says, *"...And who knows that you have come to your royal position for such a time as this. "* Then, sometime later, in chapter 9:30-31, we read about letters written by Mordecai to the Jews of the empire to confirm the days of Purim, a time established earlier to celebrate the Jews' deliverance from annihilation at an Appointed time! (Purim is still celebrated).

Ecclesiastes 3:1 (NKJV) speaks special times also: *"To everything there is a season, a time for every purpose under heaven."* God's purposes, plans, timing and place are very significant in all of scripture.

The Bible also talks about, *"The steps of a good man being ordered by the Lord: and he delighteth in his way."* (Psalm 37:23KJV)

Often I pray, "Lord, help me be in the right place at the right time." I believe when we submit our agenda to God, we give Him license to arrange our lives, with our best in mind. A person told me once, "Well, God gave you a brain to use!" That person was ridiculing me for my walk, which is to let God make choices for me. What I answered was, "Yes, He did, however, I choose to submit my brain and

57

intellect, my plans, my will and desires back to Him for a higher purpose and the greater good." What happened next after this declaration was nothing short of amazing! I began to find myself in extreme places of favor that of which I have never experienced. Some people call this "God winks" or "God bumps," but I called it miraculous. That decision to live in submission to Him opened me to an increase in divine revelation and rhema, favor, and anointing. I began to find myself in the right place at the right time, with my desired results...without even having to ask! I guess you can call that radical obedience!

How this came about in my life was the result of profound failure and some terrible circumstances. At that point I was done being a Christian (according to my agenda and will). Nothing thus far I wanted was working out, and I sat down one day and asked God to take over: to order my every step, because my way was not working, and I was tired of my life falling short. I was determined to go deeper with Him, no matter what it cost me. And it was my circumstances, people and situations around me, that propelled me to change my actions and reactions. (God doesn't change; but He will use our circumstances to help us change, for the better, and to bring mature spiritual growth).

For me, that was a place of supreme humility, like what might be needed for walking on water, or standing on Jell-O™ (12), or not knowing all the ins and outs. Soon, I began sensing Him directing me to do things differently. And every time I was obedient, there was blessing and favor. I asked Him to bind my will, heart, and mind to His, and found I was doing His will without conscious direction.

I think Esther's experiences are an example of what I experienced. Esther's heart was postured towards this kind of obedience, and hence, the king's scepter (favor) was offered to her three times in her story.

Am I perfect in this kind of walk? No. But I have known the place of extreme favor and the miraculous, and that beckons to me most of the time. I desire more of Him, more anointing, more favor, and more empowering, but it comes with a price.

But I am excited; because knowing this brings me delight anticipating what is ahead. It also increases my faith *'the substance of things hoped for and the evidence of things not seen'*, and my experiences with this walk give me eager expectation of things to come!

In Deuteronomy 28, the first third of the chapter speaks to Israel of God's blessings for obedience; the next two-thirds spell out the curses for disobedience. This indicates to me that when the Holy Spirit tells us to go right and we go left or stand still, that we remove ourselves from not just His perfect will for us, but perhaps His protection and favor. Oswald Chambers (13) said in June 20th of his My Utmost for His Highest Devotional (14a) that arguing with the Holy Spirit, our "yes- buts", actually grieves the Holy Spirit.

Perhaps you have heard the expression 'God's permissive will.' I don't buy that. I believe permissive will just amounts to asking Him to bless our will instead of His. We are given choices, for sure, but His perfect will is where we find the biggest rewards -Life. When we are in the right place, at the right time, at the appointed time in our life, then we will witness the right outcome, according to Him.

As we read, there is an appointed time for everything according to God: birth, death, etc. Again, in our quest for finding our identity in Him, we need to look for those appointed times, the "...*for such a time as this?*" (Esther 4:14) Times, for "...*in him we live and move and have our being...*" (Acts 17:28) He is the Creator (manufacturer); we are the creation (manu-factured). He knows exactly what we need.

In many ways we have lost sight of why we are here, from whence we came, and where we are going. It is not to fulfill our own ambi-tions, but to bring Him glory, to get all the spots and wrinkles out, and fulfill our destiny in Him here. This is what I believe our goals should be, and it takes submitting to God in every area of our lives… not an easy task. Our culture communicates to us early in life that we are not to be dependent, but rather independent. The world sees dependence as weakness, but God sees it as trust.

There are many levels of a Christian walk. I am saying I believe there is a place of going deeper and higher that comes with radical obedience, like Esther, who had a choice. She knew that going before the king without being invited might bring her death, because such was the custom. But her passion and love for her people, and her obedience to Mordecai her uncle (a type of the Holy Spirit) moved her to action. And then the miraculous happened: great favor to her with the King!

Meditation 11

Oh my! What are we going to do?

Life is a whirlwind right now for many! I picture people wringing their hands, shaking their heads, pacing, heads bowed, tearful, and more gray hairs forming! I see once healthy bodies showing signs of stress-induced symptoms. When you are presented with bad or hard news, do you turn to the scripture verses and Biblical principles that we have learned about God or to something else?

I read a devotional this morning describing God like a cocoon of light around us, but when we fret, like I described above, I see the cocoon developing holes, and pretty soon the light is gone and darkness prevails. What was once a light and safe place is one filled with turmoil and confusion.

Why do we destroy the Shalom He has given us? Many people believe that if they don't do X-amount of fretting, they won't have done duty in their trial. I call that 'Stinkin Thinkin'. Did you know that God does not need our help to fix our messes? But, He does call us to take charge of our thinking and speaking, and has given us the tools for that. Look at these verses:

"The world is unprincipled. It's dog-eat-dog out there! The world doesn't fight fair. But we don't live or fight our battles that way—never have and never will. The tools of our trade aren't for marketing or manipulation, but they are for demolishing that entire massively corrupt culture. We use our powerful God-tools for smashing warped philosophies, tearing down barriers erected against the truth of God, fitting every loose thought and emotion and impulse into the structure of life shaped by Christ. Our tools are ready at hand for clearing the ground of every obstruction and building lives of obedience into maturity. (2 Corinthians 10:4-6, The Message)

Do we really believe what we read? God's says in His Word that He will either take care of the problem or show us how to handle it. This is where the rubber hits the road for us with our faith. Do we believe that God's will is His will for us? Do we really connect and know that God is in us to do His will? I think most of us vacillate on this, but He tells us that His goal for us is permanent 'childlike faith'. (Matthew 18:3) What does He mean by this?

A few years ago the Lord spoke to my spirit and impressed me that He wanted me to be like my grandson Noah, who was quite young at the time. Noah never asked for food, or shelter, or protection, he just knew it would show up because he was bonded to, and was in relationship with, and trusted his par-ents. Guess what happened? He was given all that he needed without even opening his mouth to ask.

That is God's model for us: bonding with God, having relationship with Him, and knowing Him in intimate ways, and trusting Him. Do we dare believe? God does not want for us to slip in and out of that mode, but to use the tools He gives us to stay in that position so it grows and becomes part of our nature.

I am praying for some people to receive the baptism of the Holy Spirit so that God can lead them through their trials, and some seem to be waiting for a "magical moment," thinking guidance will come then. In fact, because they are believers, the Holy Spirit already dwells in them, in the form of the Holy Trinity. God in His several Persons is ready to lead and guide them because they know, and are known, by Jesus Christ. What they need is to tap into what they already have.

Are we like they are? Sometimes we need to go back to basics, to realize we have all we need to fight our battles and get our direction. In the book of Acts 2, the apostles were given the baptism of the Holy Spirit, special empowerment for the tasks ahead. However, they had already been saved and at that point they were equipped by the Jesus! It says, *" He breathed on them and they received the fullness of Christ in the form of the trinity"*. (John 20:22) Jesus then told them they were ready to do great exploits for him. The season of Pentecost is a great reminder of His empowerment given us. It is a finished work and like His early disciples, we, His disciples today, are His already and are equipped to do equally great feats.

Steep Yourself in God-Reality. He continued this subject with his disciples.

> *"Don't fuss about what's on the table at meal times, or if the clothes in your closet are in fashion. There is far more to your inner life than the food you put in your stomach, more to your outer appearance than the clothes you hang on your body. Look at the ravens, free and unfettered, not tied down to a job description, carefree in the care of God. And you count far more." (Luke12:22-24)*

Jesus answered them, "Do you finally believe? In fact, you're about to make a run for it—saving your own skins and abandoning me. But I'm not abandoned. The Father is with me. I've told you all this so that trusting me, you will be unshakable and assured, deeply at peace. In this godless world you will continue to experience difficulties. But take heart! I've conquered the world." (John 16:31-33,The Message)

In the book of Esther, when she is confronted with an intense, life or death situation, her reaction was nothing like our typical fretful ways. Instead, she called for fasting, prayer, intercession, praise, and decreeing, because she and the other Jews had been taught that was the way to respond. They acted on what they knew about God.

In Esther's day the Jews did not have the Bible as we know it, but they did have most of the Old Testament. This convinces me their response put them right in God's will, and God's will was their will. God knew them, they knew God. They trusted God and had relationship with Him. The rest is history. We are not at the mercy of our circumstances; we are beneficiaries of the mercy of God.

So set aside all that is hindering or causing stress, and practice the presence of God! Know Him, trust Him, bond with Him, be in relationship with Him, and keep that cocoon of light intact. Take captive those thoughts, those questions, those worries, and let Him carry you through whatever it is. He has not changed, does not plan on changing, and He is there in His Omnipotence and Omnipresence to fix it, or show us how to.

"Afflicted city, storm-battered, unpitied:
    I'm about to rebuild you with stones of turquoise,
Lay your foundations with sapphires,
    construct your towers with rubies,
Your gates with jewels,
    and all your walls with precious stones.
All your children will have God for their teacher—
    what a mentor for your children!
You'll be built solid, grounded in righteousness,
    far from any trouble—nothing to fear!
f ar from terror—it won't even come close!
If anyone attacks you,
    don't for a moment suppose that I sent them,
And if any should attack,
    nothing will come of it.
I create the blacksmith
    who fires up his forge
    and makes a weapon designed to kill.
I also create the destroyer—

but no weapon that can hurt you has ever been forged.

Any accuser who takes you to court

will be dismissed as a liar.

This is what God's servants can expect.

I'll see to it that everything works out for the best."

God's Decree

(Isaiah 54:11-17 The Message)

We can depend on it.

MEDITATION 12

Where is My Miracle? Part 1

Some of God's miraculous deliverances as recorded in the Bible include the following:

* Noah and his family saved from the flood in the ark, Genesis 6-8;

* Lot and his family saved from the fiery destruction of Sodom and Gomorrah, Genesis 19:29;

* Nation of Israel delivered from Egyptian slavery by the Exodus, preserved in the wilderness by miraculous care, and saved from fiery serpents by looking at a bronze serpent on a pole, Exodus 12-17;

* David and his army saved from capture by Saul's army on numerous occasions, 1 Sam 23;

* Elijah fed by the ravens in the wilderness, 1 Kings 17:2-6;

* Three young Hebrew men delivered from Nebuchadnezzar's fiery furnace, Daniel 3: 19-30;

* Daniel preserved unharmed in the lions' den, Daniel 6:1-2;

* Deliverance of the Jewish nation from Haman's plot in the Book of Esther-chapter 8.

What we can conclude from these narratives is that throughout history as we know it, God has always provided for, protected, and delivered His people. According to scripture, He is the God that changes not. However, there are many sitting in God's waiting room that has not yet been delivered. And sitting right there with them is the enemy of our soul, busily at work undermining their faith in God.

He is shooting arrows of lies into their minds: "You are being punished;" "God really does not love you;" "You are not one of His;" "He has forgotten your address;" "He loves others more than you." There is an endless stream of condemnation. Typical coward, he shoots these arrows when we are tired, hurting, and don't see an end in sight.

I saw a sign this week on a church bill board which said, "If you need a miracle, be one!"

It reminded me of a Word given to us in California, "*Take care of my people, and I will take care of you.*" As with any Rhema word (a word spoken by the Holy Spirit-our spirit), it needs to be measured against scripture for testing and proving. That time, God was true to His Word, and when we stepped outside ourselves with giving, in offerings or service He directed, He always came through!

I think that when we find ourselves in God's waiting room, instead of whining, complaining, wondering, or getting upset with God, it would be more productive to use of our time to be doing something that would make us miracles to someone else. Isn't that what Christianity is all about? The Bible says our lives should be about giving, not worrying about tomorrow, and as we seed a miracle in someone else's life, God will provide, protect, and deliver us. (There is that sow-reap principle again!)

It is all about love. Many of us, maybe from past baggage, go along in our lives with our fists up, ready to battle the world. Exhausting! Maybe in our past we had to fend for ourselves, or think that if we didn't make it happen, whatever it was, it wouldn't.

Did you know that God was there then? To paraphrase, He is saying, 'Relax, don't worry; love in my Name, give in my Name, and I will take care of all that concerns you.'

If we would get ourselves busy giving, and seeing smiles on someone else's face, we might even forget our own trials. Remember, God is love. God is an active verb, and if we have God in us, we are perhaps the only Bible some will see. So, like His Son, we, too, need to be about Our Father's business.

I can hear the objections: 'Oh, you don't understand; it is my job to do this for my family. No one else will.' That is incorrect: God loves them more that we do or can; I know how

I feel about my kids especially. To repeat the old cliché, "Let go and let God!" It's true, and some of us need to let go. He does not need us to orchestrate and implement our miracles and deliverances! The Bible has demonstrated that. As I have said, God will either fix it for us or tell us what our part is, if there is one. We need to abide within that framework.

Can you imagine what would have happened if Noah had not been obedient to build the ark, as crazy as that command must have sounded? What about Jonah in the whale? Hopefully Jonah learned about obedience so he would not become heart burn for another fish! God is amazing in His creation and His deliverance. Be careful so that we don't take ourselves out of His protection with disobedience and our own understanding.

According to the events related above, I did not see anyone asking for deliverance. In God's time-table, He just did it. The Bible demonstrates how trials and persecutions produce character and that we are being perfected for Glory. God not only wants this for our greater good, but He is also watching-us to see how we are going to handle ourselves in our trials. God always has the eternal perspective in mind, not just the short term relief we are looking for.

Take a look around the sphere of influence to see who you might be a miracle to. Do we dare look outside our own circumstances? God does not expect us to fix our calamities, because He is the expert with solutions that are beyond what we consider possible!

I think we tend to live in little compartments in our heads, but God is saying, "I am out here in a dimension you don't know about. Step outside into the area of unknown where I am!"

Be willing to prove God. He likes to show us His miraculous muscles and bring Glory to Himself. And when all is said and done, He is always on time. I believe the greater the mess, the greater the deliverance.

The Bible says," that the sun and rain fall on the just and the unjust." (Matthew 5:45) Yes, it does say that. But, the promises for deliverance and protection only fall on His, those that are known by Him and who know Him as LORD and not just Savior.

Recall Esther: once she knew what she had to do, and how treacherous it might prove for her own life, she declared, *"If I perish, I perish."*(Esther 4:16) This is an example of Esther being a miracle to others; and many miracles and favor flowed to, and was granted to her for her selfless and brave act.

So, for those of us who need miracles, perhaps a different strategy is in order while we are in God's waiting room. Delay is not denial; God is looking at our hearts and wanting to bring about eternal perspectives in us. We are so precious to Him.

The Bible also teaches that no temptation is common to man, *"...but that He will not let you be tempted beyond what you can bear..."* (1 Corinthians 10:13) Well, often we don't agree with what He thinks we can handle, however, He promises that His grace (unmerited favor), *"... is sufficient to help us bear anything..."* (2Corinthians 12: 9) So let's get busy being miracles to others while we are waiting for ours. The time will go faster in His waiting room and we won't be missing out on life!

One thing I know: God is not leaving His throne. He is in control and will never change. I don't know about you, but that knowledge brings great comfort to me. By the way, when I preach, I am doing so to myself, too, because I'm also a work in progress, also looking for miracle

MEDITATION 13

Where is my miracle? Part 2

"And a woman was there who had been subject to bleeding for twelve years, but no one could heal her. She came up behind him and touched the edge of his cloak, and immediately her bleeding stopped. "Who touched me"? Jesus asked. When they all denied it, Peter said, "Master, the people are crowding and pressing against you." But Jesus said, "Someone touched me; I know that power has gone out from me." Then the woman, seeing that she could not go unnoticed, came trembling and fell at his feet. In the presence of all the people, she told why she had touched him and how she had been instantly healed. Then he said to her, Daughter, your faith has healed you. Go in peace." (Luke 8:43-48 NIV)

I have read this text many times and I see some things going on here that released the miracle for this woman's healing: forgiveness, worship, faith, boldness, and persistence.

The woman pressed through, with great tenacity, boldness and persistence. She knew by faith Jesus held the power to heal. She contended for her healing! When she knelt down to touch the hem of his garment, it was a worshipful posture to the Savior, and so she received forgiveness. Remember, forgiveness is a choice, not a feeling!

Time brings forgetfulness. For those whose insults still persist, forgiveness and forgetfulness may need daily confession and prayer for the offending person or situation. But as you lift them up, little by little the sting goes out of the assaults and you become clean and God-released of that person.

Jesus held nothing against this woman for barging in through the crowd to touch him. It is not mentioned in scripture, but it seems as though the disciples and Jesus and the crowd could have just shoved her out of the way. But they showed her mercy and forgiveness. Jesus often forgave without the person even asking. On the cross He uttered, *"Father, forgive them, they know not what they doing."* (Luke 23:34)

Although this is not also mentioned in scripture, I see all of these qualities in Queen Esther. I wonder that, knowing what she knew about Haman's plot to kill her and her people, during her time of prayer, praise and fasting, she developed an attitude of forgiveness in her heart for him; she even invited him to a feast and broke bread with him. I believe that was the final key that unlocked the miraculous favor and deliverance in this situation. It released God to have His way. She had clean hands before the Father. Esther was merely an instrument in the right time and the right place. I wonder what the scenario would have been had her heart not been in the right place?

Examine the times we may have been falsely accused, and God calls us to forgive, regardless. This kind of forgiveness releases us from those who have hurt us and puts them into God's hand. Forgiveness and faith together, I believe, releases love, deliverance and healing...a nuclear reaction in the Spirit.

In Luke 7:47-50 the scripture describes a woman who ministered to Jesus with ointments and tears. Jesus says, *"...Therefore, I tell you, her many sins have been forgiven—as her great love has shown. But whoever has been forgiven little loves little." Then Jesus said to her, "Your sins are forgiven." The other guests began to say among themselves, "Who is this who even forgives sins?" Jesus said to the woman, "Your faith has saved you, go in peace."*

Look at verse 47, *"But whoever has been forgiven little, loves little."* As I was preparing to teach on forgiveness years ago in a women's meeting in California the Lord spoke to me through this scripture. I wonder how many people we hold captive from loving because of our un-forgiveness. One can also say, whoever has been forgiven much, loves much! When we align ourselves with this thinking, we might ask the question, 'Are we creating our own problems by making issues for the ones needing forgiveness and keeping them in bondage?' I am sure we will be held accountable before God.

We need to forgive ourselves! We need to stop beating ourselves over the head, and step out of the bondage that keeps us from loving fully. When God says forgive, we don't think that this principle also applies to us as well!

This morning I was impressed with a devotional from Oswald Chambers. He referenced Job 42:10..."*After Job had prayed for his friends, the Lord restored his fortunes and gave him twice as much as he had before.*"

Chambers' says in , 'His Utmost for His Highest Devotional'(15) that said : "If you are not getting your 'hundred-fold more', not getting insight into God's word, then start praying for your friends; enter into the ministry of the interior". The Lord turned the captivity of Job when he prayed for his friends, not just the good friends, but especially those that did not help him, and attempted to distract him.

In praying for his friends who were ill advising him in error, Job forgave them and released to himself his own recovery and deliverance. God was just waiting for this moment in Job's life, because when Job prayed for his friends, it is implied he forgave them! The next step was his recovery and redemption. It took him a while to get there. He (Job) also did not curse God during his trial, but continued in humility, prayer and praise.

I spoke to several people recently who have not received healings and deliverances yet, but the first thing I heard from all went something like this: "Why doesn't God do something? Must be miracles are not for today; God does not like me, He likes the other person better." I think the best way to avoid any questions about God's accountability or liability is to do a spiritual self-evaluation about where we fall along the line of <u>our</u> accountability. Are we lined up with His word?

Life is a process of sanctification which is designed to remove all of our "spots and wrinkles" and as I have said, God's concern is from the heavenly perspective and His Kingdom goals for our lives. He loves us too much to leave us the way we are. If, to the best of our ability, our hands are clean before Him, we should have nothing to worry about. Blaming God is counterproductive, and He is the kind of Father that only wants good gifts for His sons and daughters.

"No, well you don't understand. I must not be one of His." Yes, you are. Even our earthly parents chastise us. Many associate discipline with lack of love, or compare God with their earthly fathers. God would tell us that He can discipline His children because He loves us. His love is beyond our human comprehension; His love is unconditional and ever flowing. That is how it is between God and us.

We need to stop our thinking that borders on self-pity. God will use our trials. So we need to ask Him what the trials signify in our lives. God is the just judge and He will deal with our adversaries. And surprise! God also uses our trials and how we conduct ourselves in them for others to observe the power and glory of God manifested in our lives.

"Well, what about faith? I don't have faith?" Faith is defined in Hebrews 11:1 as *the substance of things hoped for, the evidence of things not seen.*" (NKJV) When you sit in a chair you have faith; you somehow know it is not going to fall when you sit on it. So, yes, you do a measure of faith and trust.

In a previous meditation I mentioned that many believe they don't, or won't, get their miracle because of their sense of unworthiness. Where did that come from? Why do we entertain such things? No matter who or what has told us negative things about ourselves, those words cannot stick unless we agree with them. They are contrary to God's words about us.

Some people are afraid to hope so as to avoid future disappointment. While you are trying to avoid disappointment you may actually sabotage your expected and hoped for outcome, because of the unbelief and fear. God is hope, love and faith, according to His word. So you are not actually banking on something that may or may not happen you are banking on God, the Rock, and the One who never slumbers! He is love, and, there is not fear in love. But perfect love drives out fear, because fear had to do with punishment. The one who fears is not made," *perfect in love."* (1 John 4:18)

Believe the truth that is written in scripture: "*But you are a chosen people, a royal priesthood, a holy nation, God's special possession, that you may declare the praises of him who called you out of darkness in to his wonderful light."* (1 Peter 2:9) Who would you rather believe; God or the enemy who forever wants to cut us off at the knees and keep us from what is rightfully ours?

Yes, we have been healed by the stripes He took at Calvary. But, I believe, that was our eternal healing, spiritual reconciliation with the Father, and when our earthly bodies cease, we continue living in Glory! Remember, God is sovereign and He gets to call the shots because He always is a 'bigger picture' God. When we don't get what we want, when we want it, we are to resist thinking the worst, because God sees us through blood stained lenses...and since He is the manufacturer, and we are the product, if you will, He will always know what is best for us. (Parents, does that sound familiar...having to make some tough calls with our kids and they shout back, I hate you, but they really don't!)

There is a trend with the younger generation to blame their family of origin for their issues. The truth is, we all make our own choices, and change is possible. Why is it, someone has to be blamed? And why blame God when He is not on our time schedule?

"Well, He could do this or that?" My mind cannot wrap around the workings of God, and honestly, I don't think I need to. I want to trust that even when we are stressed to the max, His grace is there for us. Sometimes I get a picture of us with a heavenly hand on our heads, and our little feet moving wildly as we dig a hole in the ground. "Stand still, says the Lord, I will work on your behalf if you let me. I will show you what your part is and I will do the rest."

These are things He as has shown me in His Word. You can find them, too. So, please, seek Him on your own, and be like the Bereans in the Book of Acts, who studied God's word, and did not just rely on what they heard. We are given keys to the kingdom. If we don't put them in the ignition and turn it over, the engines of our lives will not run. Our choice!

MEDITATION 14

Could you be stealth for God?

In the late 1990's I had a horrible car accident that forced me to see a chiropractor. Being an RN (registered nurse), I really had never considered this option; it was not congruent with my training. However, the situation warranted I try something different, a stretch for me. The chiropractor was a Christian, but was not from a denomination that moved in the gifts of the Spirit. His secretary was not a Christian at all and had New Age (15) beliefs.

The doctor did an initial x-ray and it showed that my neck was bent in a very unnatural way! During the course of my treatment I was in so much pain that he was not able to do any traditional manipulations. Instead, he used this pen-like instrument on me to try and gently move the bones in my neck. I kept asking God why I was there, and why I wasn't making any progress.

During those many visits I had ample opportunity to have conversations with the doctor and his secretary. I was only focused on my neck and back, completely unaware of anything happening at a spiritual level. However, a friend knowing my situation mentioned that she thought I might be on an 'assignment from God'. What a revelation! Her comment changed my whole perspective. I began to get my eyes off of me and on His purpose and plan in this place and with these people.

Those many conversations set the stage for me to be able to minister to him and to his secretary spiritually. One day, after I had received some personal ministry, the pain just left. The doctor did another x-ray and saw immediately that my once, abnormally bent neck, was now in a normal position! He was amazed since he knew he had not been able to do much at all because of my pain.

At my next appointment a good friend came with me and before the appointment was up, we had the privilege of praying for him for the baptism of the Holy Spirit. This was something he was not open to before, or understood. But following my testimony of my how my neck became healed, on that day, he received the Holy Spirit. In addition, I was able to get a Bible for the secretary and invited her to a women's group.

Later, another friend said to me that she believed God had sent me there as a "Stealth for Him." (The word stealth, as defined by Webster' is "an act or action of proceeding furtively, secretly, or imperceptibly, unobtrusive.") I believed that, because of my medical background I never would have chosen to see a chiropractor. But God had plans for that office and my bias did not deter Him. The accident gave me a 'legal right to be there' and minister to them. I never thought of that! This was more confirmation for me.

We believers must realize that when we ask God to use us, as we all do, do we really know what that might entail? I certainly did not. Would I have chosen this path to minister and witness to someone? No, probably not. In addition, I would not have voluntarily walked into a chiropractor's office either, without a medical necessity.

Now, we can interpret this as an example of Romans 8:28 says concerning all things working together for good. *'And we know that in all things God works for the good of those who love him, who have been called according to his purpose."*

For me having a car accident was not in my best interest, but God used it for good. God does send His servants out, and places them strategically, but unobtrusively, to do His bidding, or both. He wastes nothing.

I see this principle demonstrated in the Bible. Referencing Esther, when the King announced he was looking for a new wife, Esther was found to be amongst the fairest. In chapter 2 we read that she was taken into a women's center, along with the other virgin candidates.

After she arrived it says she immediately received the favor of Hegai, the eunuch in charge of the virgins. She underwent months of beauty and purification rituals and treatments, and we recall that when she was presented to the king later in the chapter, the king immediately was attracted to her, more than the others, and right then and there set a royal crown on her head and made her queen. She was now legal, if you will, and was strategically positioned for God. As Mordecai later stated to Esther, *"And who knows but that you have come to your royal position for such a time as this?* For if you remain silent at this time, relief and deliverance for the Jews will arise from another place, but you and your father's family will perish. And who knows but that you have come to your royal position for such a time as this?"(Esther 4:14)

In Acts 16: 16-34 Paul and Silas were imprisoned and in stocks. There was an earthquake and, to make a long story short, the jailer and his household all heard the Gospel and were saved. I am quite sure that Paul and Silas did not volunteer to be imprisoned. But if you read the story, you will see how miraculously they were released from the stocks and could have escaped, but did not. Instead, they stayed to staunch the jailer's fear, and then led the jailer and his whole household to Christ.

Scripture records other such incidents, however, here is a question; what terrible or uncomfortable situation might you be in that is actually God's plan to use you as 'stealth'? Our natural inclination is to run from these kinds of things. Or, should we dare ask God what He has for us in our trial, as opposed to take us unto HIM, and leave this planet!

We all have these choices, but I can see that when we desire to stand our ground, God will protect us and give us that grace. Not only will we complete our mission, but I believe there is blessing and healing for us because of our obedience to him.

The military uses stealth fighters, so why not the Kingdom! We are at war and Satan is a devious enemy. Let's examine and inquire of God the next time we find ourselves in some life struggle or difficult situation, whether it be at work, as a patient in a hospital, or some other uncomfortable challenge. Could you be one of God's 'stealth' fighters? Yes, you may be one. I believe this is more common than not because we are to be ready in and out of season! *"For if you remain silent at this time, relief and deliverance for the Jews will arise from another place, but you and your father's family will perish. And who knows but that you have come to your royal position for such a time as this?"* (2 Timothy 4:2)

MEDITATION 15

Feasts

Many of us can remember a worship tune based on a verse from Song of Solomon that goes, *"He brought me to the banquet hall and his banner over me is love. "* (Song of Solomon 2:4)

There are many references to feasting and feasts in the Bible. The Bible also records that Jesus' major miracles occurred during one of the many Jewish religious feasts. In fact, his first public miracle was performed at a wedding feast in Cana (John 2:1-10). Jesus is called our Bridegroom in the Book of Revelation, and there, He is preparing for us the ultimate feast, known as The Marriage Supper of the Lamb. There is much prophetic revelation for us in studying these feasts.

In the book of Esther, she is led by the Spirit to prepare two feasts for the king and Haman. The second feast becomes the venue for the Jews' deliverance from Haman's scheme of genocide. I believe this is a prophetic picture of what Jesus later goes on to tell us in the New Testament, when He admonishes us to 'feed and give drink to our enemies!' (Paraphrased-Romans12:20)

If we have spiritual ears to hear and eyes to see, we will discern that we actually already have before us at our personal feast with the

Lord. He promises us everything we need. We become a "Kingdom Now" person. In the Lord's Prayer, Jesus tells us to pray, '...*Thy kingdom come. Thy will be done in earth, as it is in heaven...*" (Matthew 6:10 KJV) What I sense many are missing is that the Kingdom is a continuum: there is the now Kingdom, where King Jesus is in-dwelling us and ruling, and the Kingdom we will enter into when we are no longer alive on this planet.

We are eternal souls! Even when our life ceases here, we immediately are alive with Him in Glory. It is not an end, it is a 'continuing,' but in a different form, to a greater Glory. And later after He returns to Earth, we are to be united with our new bodies. But for those that believe and call Him Lord, there really is no death, only transformations.

When we pray the Lord's Prayer we are calling down the Kingdom above to be the Kingdom in our dimension. If we can grasp this, then what is provided in heaven is accessible to us now. Even the principle of binding and loosing mentioned in the Bible is ours: "*Whatever is bound on earth is also bound in heaven...*" (Matthew 16:19) This principle is for our 'real time', not later.

I sense there is much we are not stepping into and possessing because we have not locked into God's principles. Remember,

God wants us to have the faith of a child that just 'knows' they will receive because of their having known and having had relationship and experience with their earthly parents. From the moment we are born, God provides for us all that is needed and required. God expects such childlike faith from us, as He is our heavenly father.

Picture a dinner table with plates of food. When we sit down we know most likely we will be in receipt of a meal, our experience tells us this. Make a mental leap to a larger table, only there are many seated all around, along with Jesus. Well, if Jesus is in us, He is at that table, too! On the plates are finances, souls, shelter, relationships, healing, protection, wisdom revelation, counsel, anointing, and so on. We can take what we need of this fare, and pass it around and bless others.

These lavishly filled plates are now being passed to us and as we partake, immediately we are filled what we want and what we need. If we want a particular delight, we say, "please pass" implying it is already on the table, we are merely accessing it. Our response usually is "thank you" and the plates continue to pass from one to the other.

What was on the plates at Esther's two feasts? Well, in Chapter 5 there was a platter of favor, and in Chapter 7, there was a platter of justice. She received by partaking. My guess is she did not even set the table, as she was royalty, and when she identified with that, she simply moved in that role, and all else was done. We need to connect with our royal status: it was given to us at the cross.

What did we do to earn this- nothing? We just sat at the table; it is part of our inheritance when we were born into the family of God! We receive because of our relationship, experience, and faith, based on our knowledge of His nature and goodness. Scripture says if we ask our earthly parents, they would never give us a snake or stone. *"...How much"* *more would our heavenly Father give us 'good* *gifts?"* (Matthew 7:9-11) I think this gives a whole new perspective to what we are entitled to as believers, and honestly, it has shown me that when I pray, rather than ask, I will simply thank Him for what I believe I have in the Spirit that will soon manifest in the natural.

Instead of begging and pleading, I enter into intercession with thanks. We need to make connection with the fact that as believers, we are members of a royal family and it comes with royal privileges, and authority. *We need* *to let this premise* permeate every fiber of our being. Our inheritance is tied into being part of that, *"...royal priesthood and chosen gener-* *ation..."* (1 Peter 2:9) We are made in *"...His image and likeness...* " (Genesis 1:27) that is no small thing.

Meditating on these principles has freed me to minister to others, 'knowing' that as I take care of His people; He will take care of me. I have had many 'God Winks' to confirm this revelation to me, i.e. providing something I needed or wanted without seeking it out myself.

I also know that this blessing comes because I seek to be obedient to His Spirit. *Faith + obedience + humility= Resurrection Power.* Do I get all I want? No. I am submitted to the fact that, as He is the creator and I am the creation, He may reserve the right to withhold something that is not in my best interest. We must realize that what we may interpret as rejection is simply His protection.

All He gives us in this Kingdom is not just to make us 'fat and happy', but to equip us to propagate the Kingdom of God in this age. God is raising up marketplace apostles to invest in the Kingdom and expand it. The Bible also says,"..., *to whom much is given, much is required. But the one who does not know and does things deserving punishment will be beaten with few blows. From everyone who has been given much, much will be demanded; and from the one who has been entrusted with much, much more will be asked.* " (Luke 12:48)

Time for a paradigm shift!

Next time you sit at a table to eat, as you look at the plate, shift gears and envision what He has for you at His table, what is there for the taking: it is not just food! He has all we need already on the table, ready for us to partake! Dare we believe!

Praying (talking to God) with this new-found authority for me or others has brought much fruit. We all tend to be self-centered in some way or another, but what I see the Bible saying is that it is about doing for others, laying our lives down, not scrambling to make things happen for ourselves which can occupy too much of our mental and spiritual energy.

The banqueting table is set now; we can partake and be filled. It is here because of His great love for us and His great sacrifice for us that He made over 2000 years ago. When we pass from this glory to the next, it will be only the blink of an eye, and indeed, I believe will be the greatest feast ever!

Wanting to make the most of our lives here and stepping into our inheritance, rather than entertaining a poverty mentality, is what I believe He wants us to have. The time is now!

Again, this is a revelation given to me and I really think it is a Word for the Body of Christ to rise up and take the land.

"From the days of John the Baptist until now the kingdom of heaven has suffered violence, and the violent take it by force." (Matthew 11:12 KJV)

Let us aspire to a higher place in our vision and callings with Him. I believe we will see Him working mightily in our lives.

MEDITATION 16

Healing Practices that bring healing your way

I was thinking of healing last week and all the different types we see in the Bible: spiritual, physical, emotional, financial, and political (as in the book of Esther). Then there is perfect healing, His perfect healing occurs when we are reunited with our Maker and given a new body! One way or the other for the believer, healing is part of our inheritance. It is God's will.

There are many healings in God's waiting room too, waiting in line to be dispatched. You may wonder why some people get healed now, and some not till the journey home. I don't know, however, I do know that God does not waste anything, and His sovereign nature dictates when: now or later.

While I don't believe there are magic prayers or formulas to get God to move His hand in healing, there are many Scriptures that allude to when healing may appear, or when we are ripe for healing. I have experienced some myself along these lines. I have had chronic back pain since 1996, the result of a work injury. Two years ago I fractured my pelvis and became somewhat of a 'couch potato' out of necessity, to promote healing in those bones. Unfortunately, the immobility which allowed my pelvis to heal caused my chronic back issues even more insult, and the muscles in my body began to weaken, so I began to fatigue easily. The end result was just more inescapable pain.

I decided to try and start walking again. Previously, I could not last ten minutes without excruciating pain. In my heart I was determined to be able to walk again the way I used to, and one particular morning I told my husband, "I think you have to push past the pain for healing to come." I thought about the birth of my two children and how I had to push past the pain to facilitate their birth! There was no escape from that either.

I kept pondering this in my spirit and next thing you know the Lord began birthing a message. So I am going to enumerate some things that I feel the Lord was showing me that will generate excited expectation (hope) that "...*the Sun of righteousness will appear with healing in His wings...*" (Malachi 4:2)

First: Bless and praise the Lord in all we do!

"*Praise the LORD, my soul; all my inmost being, praise his holy name. Praise the LORD, my soul, and forget not all his benefits—who forgives all your sins and heals all your diseases.*" (Psalm 103:1-3)

Be postured in worship *"...the woman with the issue of blood had to bend down to touch the hem of his garment...",* and faith she knew He had been healing many, and she did not even to ask, just touched. (Luke 8:43-48) I believe her faith and persistence, pushing past the crowd, activated the healing anointing in Jesus. For myself, I was reaching out to "touch His hem", and what that looked like for me was picking up my guitar and worshipping Him every day until my breakthrough.

Second: Become acquainted with the intimate knowledge of His love, i.e. the secret place, and abiding under the shelter of His wings.

> *"Surely he will save you from the fowler's snare and from the deadly pestilence."* (Psalm 91:3)

> *"Because he loves me,"* says the LORD, *"I will rescue him; I will protect him, for he acknowledges my name. He will call on me, and I will answer him; I will be with him in trouble, I will deliver him and honor him. With long life I will satisfy him and show him my salvation."* (Psalm 14-16)

Third: Be and identify with what He did on Calvary for you.

> *"But He was wounded for our transgressions, he was bruised for our*

iniquities: the chastisement for our peace was upon him, and with his stripes we are healed." (Isaiah 53:5 KJV)

Fourth: Revere His Name.

"But for you who revere my name, the sun of righteousness will rise with healing in its rays. And you will go out and frolic like well-fed calves." (Malachi 4:2)

Fifth: Continue groaning and pushing and crying out through the pain.

"Then they cry unto the Lord in their trouble, and he saveth them out of their distresses. He sent his word and healed them, and delivered them out from their destructions." (Psalm 107:19-20.KJV)

"We know that the whole creation has been groaning, as in the pains of childbirth, right up to the present time. Not only so, but we ourselves, who have the firstfruits of the Spirit, groan inwardly as we wait eagerly for our adoption to sonship, the redemption of our bodies. For in this hope we were saved. But hope that is seen is no hope at all. Who

*hopes for what they already have?
But if we hope for what we do not
yet have, we wait for it patiently."*
(Romans 8: 22-25)

Sixth: Make Jesus Lord of your life. What this means to me is that you include Him on all decisions and allow Him to lead, guide, and direct your every step: no more picking and choosing what you want to include Him in. Practice radical obedience.

*"Once you were alienated from God
and were enemies in your minds
because of your evil behavior. But
now he has reconciled you by
Christ's physical body through
death to present you holy in his
sight, without blemish and free from
accusation-..."* (Colossians 1:21-22)

Seventh: Speak life to yourself.

Proverbs 18:21 talks about death and life being in the power of the tongue, and Romans 4:17 talks about speaking those things that are not as though they are-(paraphrased). We all have choices with our words, and I myself have caught myself saying things like, "Oh, such and such is killing me," etc. The Bible says that our bodies listen to us. The Spirit is also subject to the master!

Eighth: The anointing of God is on your life and you must protect it at all cost and be submersed in His presence.

> *"It shall come to pass in that day that his burden shall be taken away from your shoulder, And his yoke from your neck, And the yoke will be destroyed because of the anointing oil."* (Isaiah 10:27.NKJV)

MEDITATION 17

What is our response when the king beckons?

Esther Chapter 1: 3-22 is a loaded chapter that I believe applies to us all! King Ahasuerus had a feast; his queen, Vashti, also had a feast. While she was busy with the women, the King summoned her through his eunuchs, but she refused to come. The scripture said in verse 12 that the king was furious and his anger burned within him.

The concern of the day, besides publically refusing the king, was that her behavior would be observed by the empire's women and possibly instigate them to rebellion and excessive contempt, and wrath as well (verses 17-18).

What do we do when the King calls us?

What does He do if we won't come?

There are endless excuses: here are a few.

You say, Well, I don't know what God wants me to do? I don't hear God's voice...For those that cannot hear or interpret God's Rhema Word which is communication that is spoken to our spirit by the Holy Spirit, let me remind you that what He wants us to do is clearly laid out in His Word. However, if you don't read it, you won't know His Will.

You say, I have been meaning to read the Word, but I have not gotten around to it. None of us are guaranteed tomorrow, so if we suddenly end up before His throne, I am not sure that excuse will hold water.

You say I don't have a Bible. We live in the free world; there are plenty around, even free ones, so get one!

You say I don't hear God the way I used to... Perhaps there is static on your line because of sin. Complacency is the road to death.

There is a saying that ignorance will lead to bliss. But in God's Kingdom we are not only accountable for what we read, but also for failing to do what we read! *"Faith without works [Godly response]) is dead."* (James 2:17, [paraphrased])

You say You don't understand, I am eternally secure...I respectfully would have you read John 15, Hebrews 6, and Deuteronomy 28 for starters, and decide after you read those if that is true. There have been many Godly people that fell from grace, and in some instances I think, have almost resembled Vashti's situation.

There is a story I have heard about Reinhard Bonnke (16), a very powerful, in-the-spirit man of God. The way the story goes is the anointing that is now Reinhardt's, was for another, who did not want what God had for him. So, the calling and gift was passed to Reinhardt (just like Vashti's crown was passed to Esther). Need I say more? I wonder what that man is going to say when he gets before the King and is asked why he did not want what God had for him.

You say but you don't understand. I can't do that. I can't preach-I am a nobody. God does not call the qualified, He qualifies the called. Look at Moses the leader of Israel, who was a murderer and stutterer; look at King David the giant killer, who was the youngest of his family; look at Saul the Pharisee who became Paul the Apostle; look at what God did with Peter the fisherman. I have seen it in the Bible many times. It is saying yes to God, and He does the rest.

Scripture says that God looks at the attitudes of the heart in terms of willingness, and He provides all a person needs to move on to do great exploits in Him.

Now, let's look at what happens when you won't come when called. Let's start with Jonah, whom God called to go preach repentance to the city of Nineveh. Instead of obeying, he went the other way and ended up taking in the belly of a whale. Oh, he eventually got there, but what a price to pay.

Let's return to Vashti. She was REPLACED. That can happen, too, when you refuse the

King. In Deuteronomy 28 God enumerates the blessings He has prepared for obedience to His Law. But in the last half of the chapter He lays out the curses for disobedience.

You say that's the Old Testament; we are under grace... If God did not want us to read and learn from the examples of the Old Testament, it would not be part of the Bible. Using both is called preaching the full gospel of Christ. Both Christ and the Apostles regularly referred to the Scriptures.

It all boils down to this question: have you made Jesus Lord of your life? This means that He gets to be involved in everything and direct all. As I have said before, there is a place of extreme blessing and favor for obedience and submitting to His Lordship in all areas of our lives. That should be coveted by every Christian.

The Bible says that the Lord is patient and has a long fuse, but He does have a limit. Genesis 6:3 shows that His Spirit will not strive with man forever.

Matthew 3:12 says "with the winnowing fork in His hand He will separate the wheat from the chaff;" Matthew 24:24 says, "In the last days, even His elect, (persevering Christians) may be deceived."

This is a tough message. When God calls and says jump, it pays for us to say "how high?"

I urge you to test the spirits; be Bereans and seek to know what the truth is, because *"the truth will set you free."* (John 8:32)

Our goal is holiness and eternity. I think the record about Vashti is not there for just understanding how Esther became queen. It is a terrible picture of what may happen to us if we harden our hearts and don't come when called. Matthew 4:9 exhorts us *"let us have ears to hear what the Spirit is saying."*

I am going to close with some words I read this morning from Oswald Chambers' July 18th meditation in My Utmost for His Highest (18)-

"But woe be to me if when I see Him and I say- I *will* not. He will never insist that I do, but I have begun to sign the death warrant of the Son of God in my soul. When I stand face to face with Jesus Christ and say- I will not, He will never insist; but I am backing away from the re-creating power of His Redemption. It is a matter of indifference to God's grace how abominable I am if I come to the light; but woe to me if I refuse the light. (See John 3:19-21)

God loves us too much to leave us the way we are. But know also that judgement will start with the body of Christ for sure...1 Peter 4:17.

MEDITATION 18

Joy Comes in the Morning

Last night was kind of rough; I received some devastating news about a loved one and cried myself to sleep. Before we were ready to sleep my husband did not say his traditional, 'I love you, Jo'. Instead he said, "God is love. I have God in me, so 'I God you', Jo." I thought that was very insightful and it led me to begin to think about faith and hope as well.

This morning, while I was out for my walk I was reminded of *Psalm 30:5: "For His anger is for a moment, and His Favor for life; Weeping may endure for the night, but joy comes in the morning."* It made me realize that I was indeed glad for the morning and also noticed that I was infused with hope, even though nothing had changed the situation.

The Bible talks a lot about hope. Webster describes it as "excited expectation."

My outlook this morning indeed had changed. Instead of the sadness I went to sleep with, I now had hope. As Dave had pointed out, I have God inside me, so that new hope in me wasn't me, but was actually God-in-me! Then, following the logic one step further, I realized that I have the whole package inside me: faith, hope, and love, because He resides in me with all that He is! I was so thankful to Him for uplifting me, even when I was not aware. And I recalled Colossians 1:27, which says, "*To them God willed to make known what are the riches of the glory of this mystery among the Gentiles, which is Christ-in-us, the hope of Glory.*"

I know right now there are many persons sitting in God's waiting room waiting for answers. Often I hear, "but I don't have the faith." Realize that if we have Jesus inside us, then we do have the faith necessary...the Faith of Jesus. Somehow, it seems we think we have to experience some kind of feeling in order to believe we have faith, hope, or love. It is not a feeling, it is reality!

I want to encourage those who are challenged with difficult situations. All that is necessary to traverse our mountains is already within us in the person of Jesus Christ. Even when our mouths cannot utter, our spirits are enabled with Him inside of us.

There's more. The joy of the Lord is there also, to give us strength when <u>we</u> are weak. With Him inside we are complete to meet the challenges of our days, so we should not be dependent on our feelings.

Born again believers should stand on the knowledge that Christ is inside of us. He is the power source for each day, for working out our situations, even when we cannot see or feel it. He is the God that never slumbers!

For me, from last night when I closed my eyes, to this morning, circumstances were no different. But I am so happy and grateful that when I was sleeping, God-in-me was encouraging me and strengthening me in my spirit. Indeed, joy had come in the morning.

Remember this: it may be a fact that we FEEL faithless or hopeless, but it is the devil working through our emotions to deceive us about our spiritual potential. If Jesus Christ is resident in our hearts, then we can stand on the reality of what is written in Romans 8:26-27: *"The Spirit makes utterance in us when our mouths are not even speaking."* God is at work! Be encouraged!

MEDITATION 19

Game Changers for God!

When reading about Esther it is very clear she was a Biblical times Game Changer! She set the bar pretty high when she went with her gut and approached the King without being summoned; but she was willing to take a chance for the greater good, that of saving her people.

I think a modern-day female game changers might include, but not be limited to, Aimee Semple McPherson (18), founder of the Four Square Church (19) which is still going strong to this day. She was not an obvious choice for leadership since she was twice divorced and female, and basically an unknown. But she answered the call and made an enormous impact. I saw a poster on Facebook not too long ago that said, "God does not call the qualified, but qualifies the called." How about Kathryn Kuhlman (20) or Maria Woodsworth-Etter (21); Smith Wigglesworth (22) started out as a plumber!

Then there is King David. He was the youngest and most inexperienced in his family, but later killed a giant and became king. He had some odd characteristics, too, like dancing in his underwear before the Lord. Did he have sin in his life? It is recorded: yes. He committed adultery and also pre-meditated murder. But his heart was toward God and he did repent, though there was a cost.

I think God loves people that are 'out there' and unafraid to be different.

Moses stuttered and also murdered a man; Peter was an ordinary fisherman, Paul an accessory to murder. And the woman at the well, also in adultery, became the first woman evangelist. What about Rahab the harlot, ended up in the lineage of Jesus!

So, I started thinking about what it means to be a game changer for God.

Let us look at some of the qualities evident in the lives of game changers for God. They made history and changed it up for all of us.

- Available and being in the right place at the right time...Esther 4:14- *"For if you remain silent at this time, relief and deliverance for the Jews will arise from another place, but you and your father's family will perish. And who knows but that you have come to your royal position for such a time as this?"*

A whole nation was saved when she stepped out in obedience, bravery and boldness.

- Poor in spirit...Matthew 5:3-

"Blessed are the poor in spirit, for theirs is the kingdom of heaven."

Are you feeling poor in spirit? That means there is much room for the Holy Spirit in you. Rejoice: you are ripe for possessing the land as a game changer!

· Chance takers/Adventurous...
  1 Samuel 17:50-

"So David triumphed over the Philistine with a sling and a stone; without a sword in his hand he struck down the Philistine and killed him."

Mind you, the story relays he was given Saul's armor and he decided to take it off because it was too cumbersome. But he had boldness and a spirit of adventure, and trust in God, and he declared before he killed Goliath that the battle was the Lord's, and that He would be his armor.

When God promotes, He provides. I heard in a documentary one time that the velocity that David's the stone traveled in order to penetrate Goliath's forehead, and the exact spot it had to hit, was nothing short of miraculous. Can't you see the angel of the Lord Himself, Jesus Christ, escorting that speeding stone to the desired spot to knock out the giant so

David could go and cut off his head? All David had to do was take that step, and God did the rest!

It was the same for Moses facing the Red Sea with the Egyptians hotly pursuing. The Red Sea did not part until Moses took one step into it.

What steps is God calling you to take? Is He calling you to step up to the plate so He can knock it out of the park for you?

· Visionary/ Having Heaven's perspective...

Look through the windshield, not the rear view mirror.

> *"Therefore, if anyone is in Christ, the new creation has come: the old has gone, the new is here!* "(2 Corinthians 5:17)

The Christian walk is all about change. I heard someone say one time, "If you are not changing, you must be dead." We need to lay our lives on the altar, as even Abraham did. He was called to sacrifice the most precious thing in his life, his son. Isn't that what God did for us! Sometimes God calls us to lay everything down, only to give it all back, and then some. Abraham became the father of nations. God wants to fill us with new wine, but we have to get rid of the old wineskin.

He is looking for those who want to move on, without reservations.

> *"See, I am doing a new thing! Now it springs up; do you not perceive it? I am making a way in the wilderness and streams in the wasteland."*
> (Isaiah 43:19)

· Willing to step out of the box/forerunner/no matter what anyone says... Genesis 6:13-

"So God said to Noah, "I am going to put an end to all people, for the earth is filled with violence because of them. I am surely going to destroy both them and the earth."

Can you imagine the chiding and comments he got when he begin building an ark? But he was focused and determined to complete the ark.

· Prophetic/ knows God's heart on the matter /when God says jump, they say, how high? (1 Kings 18)

Elijah was facing the prophets of Baal, all 400 against him. When I read the story I could not see anywhere God telling Elijah specifically what to do. However, He knew the heart of God in preparing for the battle. Remember, it was God's reputation that was at stake. How often do we challenge Him to glorify Himself in our situations? One would look at Elijah and think he was nuts to take this on, however I believe he knew beyond a shadow of a doubt what he would do, and what would happen.

We are all called to prophesy, to 'know God's heart on the matter', in fact the scripture says, *"Where there is no vision,* (which when translated, means prophetic revelation), *the people will perish..."* (Proverbs 29:18 KJV)

We are not perfect people; do you have something that needs fixing in your life? John 9:1 says Jesus *"...saw a man blind from birth. His disciples asked him, "Rabbi, who sinned, this man or his parents, that he was born blind? Neither this man nor his parents sinned, said Jesus, but this happened so that the works of God might be displayed in him."*

This man got healed. It does not say what happened to him after, but one can speculate he told anyone and everyone of his miracle. He became an evangelist, like the woman at the well. I have heard Christians say the reason this or that is not well in your life is because you don't have enough faith, or there's sin in your life. This scripture illustrates that sin was not an issue, or in his genes. There are reasons for everything in the Kingdom of God.

I believe that the trials and persecutions that Jesus says we will have in our lives are opportunities for miracles and potential ministries, offering qualities and character, lessons and compassion we would not have known any other way.

Do you see yourself with any of these qualities? Is God calling you to be a game changer? We all have purpose and destiny. We are here for a reason, and I dare say, not to just earn a living and survive. We should seek His face to know what that may be with all that we have in us. Grab hold of the horns of the altar, and look through the windshield, as I said, not the rear view mirror. For some, the past are like cement shoes weighting us down. But the song- "Break Every Chain©" (23) says, "There is power in the Name of Jesus to break every chain..."

"With God, all things are possible."
(Matthew 19:2)

So, as you go about your days, know that God is calling game changers up to the plate for Himself, take that step and He will knock it out of the park! Will you say, "Yes, Lord." These are difficult times; they are calling for people with the above qualities to be used for God's Glory.

Yes, Lord, *"as for me and my house, we will serve the Lord!"*
(Joshua 24:15)

MEDITATION 20

Greater Things: What is your platform?

"Believe me when I say that I am in the Father and the Father is in me; or at least believe on the evidence of the works themselves. Very truly I tell you, whoever believes in me will do the works I have been doing, and they will do even greater things than these, because I am going to the Father." (John 14:11-12)

> *"Believe me: I am in my Father and my Father is in me. If you can't believe that, believe what you see— these works. The person who trusts me will not only do what I'm doing but even greater things, because I, on my way to the Father, am giving you the same work to do that I've been doing. You can count on it. From now on, whatever you request along the lines of who I am and what I am doing, I'll do it. That's how the Father will be seen for who he is in the Son. I mean it. Whatever you request in this way, I'll do.* (John 14:11-12 The Message)

What I see in these verses is a mandate to us to not only to carry on Jesus' work on this earth, but His expectation that it will be greater in both size and dimension than what He did. My mind has a hard time grabbing a hold of *"greater"* than what He did." However, the Kingdom of God is always moving forward ...not in reverse. I think we have no idea what is ahead in magnitude of His works as He ushers in the next great move of God in our time. Creation is groaning for that now! We are ripe!

There are some basic Biblical conditions that put us in the place of receiving what God has for us; obedience, faith, integrity, humility, worship, praise, forerunner spirit, tenacity, persistence. And there is another. Remember, in a previous meditation I spoke of the 'legal right' to be in a certain circumstance. In the natural, this is when you are the authorized person for a certain work, job, or position. But this right (ordained and enabled by God) also will enable you to function in that place as "a stealth" for Him. These are some of the things we have discussed before in previous meditations, mirrored in Biblical personalities, such as Esther.

From that perspective, let's move to the concept of 'platform.' I will define platform: for all practical purposes, it is a place where God puts us and ordains, anoints, and appoints us to be. Some of these places may be glamorous, some of them not. When we are in that place, He gives us all that we need to advance in His

Kingdom and to advance the Kingdom. It is a place, as with Esther, *'for such a time as this'*; where she was given favor and anointing, which is supernatural power and wisdom, along with everything she needed, to be used to save her people. When she accepted the assignment, she came into agreement with the plans and purposes of God. In this place, there was no limit to her potential and she was jettisoned into action, victory, and fulfillment.

So, as believers we are mandated to be alert to, and to search for and seek that place of our anointing in His Kingdom. Along with salvation comes the command to be a follower of Jesus Christ. To me, there is no greater rush in this world than being touched by the manifest presence of God. So many come to Jesus thinking that is the way to escape hell. But they miss the fullness and fulfillment that awaits them in walking with Jesus Christ. Also, many get saved and become consumed with building their own kingdoms of family or career. Don't get me wrong, all those are excellent things, but they are not always God's priorities for advancing the Kingdom in our life. We are here for Him, not for us! He is the Creator and we are the created, and I think that fact is often ignored.

In your platform place, there is authority, favor, and protection, as we have seen with Esther, David, Paul, Moses, Elijah, and Elisha.

Not only that, Elisha, Elijah's protégé, asked for and received a double portion of his teacher's anointing in order to advance God's Kingdom.

What is your platform? There was a great movie that came out around 2007 called, "Facing the Giants". (25) There were many great lessons in this movie, but one of the things that struck me was that the coach, he was the main character facing challenges on all fronts of his life. He was a high school football coach with a wife, a broken down truck, a failing team, financial problems, and so on.

He was a Christian who was honestly wanting to get things right, but was only beating his head against a wall because he was trying to make things happen on his own. Overwhelmed, he gave up. At that point of surrender, God sent a prophetic word to him and what it amounted to was for him to 'bloom where he was planted'.

Though he faced all these obstacles, after God adjusted his heart attitude and he was able to accept God's platform, God quickly launched him. He got everything he needed and then some! He began to praise and taught others the importance of praise; he saw that it was not so much that you win, but how you played the game. Every single area of his life became victorious as he experienced the abundance of God's grace. As Ephesians 3:20

states, *"He is able to do exceedingly and abun-dantly, above what we ask or think, according to the power that works within us"*. (NKJV)

I cannot do justice to the many significant Biblical principles in this film, but because this coach had not only found his platform, he used it for God's glory, and God rewarded him.

In scripture we are called to be lights in a dark world. Well, even a lamp has a 'platform' to shine from! *"You are the light of the world. A town built on a hill cannot be hidden. Neither do people light a lamp and put it under a bowl. Instead they put it on its stand, and it gives light to everyone in the house. In the same way, let your light shine before others, that they may see your good deeds and glorify your Father in heaven."* (Matthew 5:14-16)

Perhaps you are in a place where there are things you would rather do, or want to do? I would challenge all of you to run it by the 'Throne of Grace'. Ask, 'Is this my platform, Father?' Or, maybe you are struggling with your job, which is your platform) but in your heart you want to run away.

I think God may be waiting for us to joyfully surrender to Him in our hearts. That single decision will unlock His power that enables us to *"...run the race set before us."* (Hebrews 12:1) When we step up to the plate, we will watch Him knock it out of the ballpark. Heart attitude is so important. He puts us in places sometimes that may even be dark, but they are places where our lives are the only Bible someone may see, and that is far more powerful than any spoken or written words.

Did you know that there are great ministers who have ventured into territories that were not their platform in order to expand their ministries, but they met with failure? Why, because, God wanted them to focus on one certain area. Billy Graham (25) was one. When he realized this, he returned to where he and God had started, and the sky was the limit. He is one of the spiritual giants of our time.

Think about where you are and what your platform is to advance the Kingdom. That needs to be the main focus of your life. President John F. Kennedy (26) said it the best at his inaugural speech: "Ask not what your country can do for you, ask what you can do for your country." (27) I believe that we not only need to ask God what we can do for Him, but where we are to do it. I believe even with the most meager platforms, we all have a part to play in advancing the Kingdom and we experience God equipping and launching us to do those greater things that He has mandated and spoken we will do! How exciting! Bloom where you are planted or, find your place of planting in Him and watch and see Him light you up for the whole world to see.

MEDITATION 21

The Journey

I have been re- reading *"Hinds Feet in High Places" (28)* by Hannah Hurnard. (29) It is an awesome allegory with profound spiritual insights into purpose, our journey, and victory for the believer. Many of us can put ourselves in the main character's shoes: her name is Little Much Afraid, and Jesus is referred to as the Chief Shepherd. She lives in the Valley of Humiliation in the village of Trembling Fear as a member of the Fearling Family. I am sure that from her location and family name, you can get a handle on what her issues and baggage might be.

I think the most important point in this story is the power of God's love and the yearning for that love in all of our hearts. Also, we learn that acquiring this love comes with a price tag; it's no different than Jesus experienced when He died on the cross for us. Little Much Afraid's progression and journey demonstrate the power of sorrow and suffering in our lives, and how it not only produces character, but is actually used by God to propel us forward and upward.

The book also talks about how, in the journey upward to the High Places, there are many enemies and obstacles to face, and how

God is available to deliver us when we cry out to Him. In Psalm 107:6 we see repeatedly the phrase, "...*and then they cried out to Him, and He delivered them.*"

By the end of the book, Little Much Afraid's name, by choice, is transformed into Grace and Glory. The companions she feared, Sorrow and Suffering, were embraced along the way, and helped her to defeat the enemies in her life, especially Fear and Pride. Her companions carried her and directed her to the High Places and she was healed inside and out. And Jesus, with her permission, planted the Seed of Love in her heart. (It did cause a slight pang when he placed it in her heart). So, the onset of the journey blossomed into Christ's love. At the very end the former Little Much Afraid goes back to the Valley of Humiliation to save her family, only this time, she has been perfected in love and no longer has Fear, hence her name-change to Grace and Glory.

My description does not give full justice to this little book; however it gave me many perspectives and brought much healing into my life. We are all going through some kind of challenge and many are living in the Village of Much Trembling in the Valley of Humiliation, where Little Much Afraid lived. It inspires us to realize that though we are in service to the Chief Shepherd, as she was, there are higher heights, and that with His help, and by

PROPHETIC MEDITATIONS ON ESTHER

embracing our sorrows and suffering instead of trying to run from them, we can be perfected in His love and receive healing and grace and glory.

Being Christian is not just about getting ready for eternity; it is about maximizing our lives in this earthly part of Kingdom now. Are we going to be satisfied with just the mundane, or will we move on to our higher purpose and calling, and be perfected in the great love that He has for us?

As I read this book I think about our Biblical forefathers and see there is a parallel between their journeys and Little Much Afraid's journey. I recall outstanding examples of how Jesus took some fisherman and made them great apostles. Were their journeys easy? No. But they began with an act of willingness, and a desire for the 'Higher Places'. When the apostles arrived, there were signs and wonders following that impacted their sphere of influence and even us today! The list is endless: Samson, Job, Esther and David. Our God is "...*the God that does not change...*" (Paraphrased-Malachi 3:6) Each one of those people had a hunger for more and God met them at their place of need and desire.

Where are we on our journey to the Higher Places? Are we being scared off the path by fear, or bondage, from past hurts, pride and complacency? There is a way out of our Valleys of Humiliation and our Villages of Much Trembling. There is healing from our past hurts and disfigurements, whether figurative or literal. It starts with desire, moves on to reaching out to God, letting Him plant the Seed of Love, being willing to be made vulnerable, and being willing to love as He did.

Real love comes with a cost. It is not some icky, sticky, romantic, emotional experience. It is the act of laying down one's life to make a difference in someone else's life, as our leader Jesus did by example. Could we jump on a mine to save our partner, like a Marine (30) in Afghanistan did? It is not all about pain, but it is about perfection. His perfect love casts out all fear.

Do we really want to get well? That's a probing question. I bet the man at the Pool of Bethesda (John 5:1-15) thought about that. He had been there for years, lame and making the most of alms that was given to him. But, there is a better way. There is direction –a path and help to get to the 'Higher Places', and even healing. The man at the pool took Jesus' hand and I believe that act propelled him in to his healing.

I want to go higher with Him. I want to be perfected in love. Even as I look at a beautiful rose, it is always accompanied with thorns.

Christ is calling us to stay on the path with Him to the Higher Places, to keep our eyes focused on Him, and not to give up, no matter what our circumstances. Does He take all the thorns away? Maybe and maybe not. God knows what we need to stay on our path with Him. He is with us on that path.

> "LORD, the God of Israel, there is no God like you in heaven above or on earth below—you who keep your covenant of love with your servants who continue wholeheartedly in your way." (2 Chronicles 6:1)

This inspires me to hope that I don't have to wait to get to heaven to be an instrument of His love and be transformed into Grace and Glory.

> "I press on toward the goal to win the prize for which God has called me heavenward in Christ Jesus." (Philippians 3:14)

The Message says this passage in another way: "*I'm not saying that I have this all together, that I have it made. But I am well on my way, reaching out for Christ, who has so wondrously reached out for me. Friends, don't get me wrong: By no means do I count myself an expert in all of this, but I've got my eye on the goal, where God is beckoning us onward—to Jesus. I'm off and running and I'm not turning back."* (Philippians 3:14)

Can you relate? I can. Who wants to be rid of baggage and fear? Reach out to Him today. His hand is extended to you!

> *"There is no fear in love. But perfect love drives out fear because fear has to do with punishment. The one who fears is not made perfect in love."* (1 John 4:18)

MEDITATION 22

Disturbed

Are you disturbed?

While I was out doing my prayer walk this morning, I began to ask,

Am I disturbed, if so, why? What are the kinds of disturbances in our lives?

I see two kinds:

First, that which comes when we focus on our circumstances, which automatically moves is away from our "ignorance is bliss" mode, and fall into challenge of reality.

Second, when God rocks our boat and disturbs our comfort zones in order to either re-direct us, or to get our attention.

I think it is important to distinguish between these, because we may miss something if we chalk it all up to the devil, circumstances, or bad choices. I believe God does not waste anything in our lives and if we would be as spiritually tuned into Him as we are to our smart phones, tablets, computers or what have you, we would be able to stay on track with Him.

Let's look at the first cause. Our peace can be based on ignorance, or, when we pour buckets of carnal anesthesia over our sticky situations in order to keep steady on our courses. Neither of these will it solve our issues. In fact, my experience teaches me that they grow bigger and bigger because temporal efforts are futile. Problems are still there after a movie, or TV show, or dinner, drinks, or whatever.

The only true peace is the kind that comes from Him. *"Peace I leave with you; my peace I give you."* (John 14:27) It is implied in this scripture that there are copious amounts of peace available to us when we focus on Him. So, why do we go elsewhere? When we go to temporal places, the results are temporary at best, and the result is that we become exceptionally 'disturbed'.

An illustration of the second possibility, that God wants to get our attention, might look like the following. We are going about our lives: great car, house, jobs, kids, finances all plumb, and then, all of a sudden it the bottom drops out on us. The job is gone, fire took the house, etc. and we come unglued. Did you know that God allows trials to come into our lives to wake us up? His purpose may be to cause us to place Him back on the throne of our life, or to lead us to His desired destiny for us (which He had all along until we selected what we think He wants for us.) Be assured, He will come and rock the boat till we get the memo, because He loves us. Some people don't like change! Watch out! You are guaranteed change, so prepare yourselves!

I wonder what was going on in Esther's life before the king decided he needed a new queen. Could she have known her life, whatever it was, was about to be interrupted and disturbed... for a nation? In due course, she left her uncle's home to live in a harem where she spent twelve months being prepared for just the possibility of becoming queen. But she did not know for sure that she would be the next queen. It must have felt like trying to stand on Jell-O™. Her whole life had been like a puzzle suspended in midair, with no clue what it would look like when it hit the ground. She had been disturbed by God, so her present and future suddenly became uncertain. Nonetheless, I believe she had the Shalom of God with her in the process!

When Jesus called His disciples, their lives were interrupted and they became disturbed with His command, *"...Follow Me, and I will make you fishers of men."* (Matthew 4:19 NKJV)

What about Jonah? He did not want to go to Nineveh, so to help him become obedient; God provided him a detour in the belly of the whale!

There are many other examples in scripture and I am sure the peace of these spiritual pillars was royally rocked. Yet, in all of them, I know His peace was available to minister to all, and based on their behavior, I would say that they accepted the peace He gives in order to complete their callings without falling apart.

Some of us are tough nuts to crack! Don't you realize that the attitude of "my way or no way," is a recipe for disaster? Remember Shadrach, Meshach, and Abednego in the fire? They had the Prince of Peace present with them! (Daniel 3:24-25)They made it through a fiery furnace unblemished and rejoicing! Having the Prince of Peace present in our trials is all part of our inheritance. Why would we not want to accept Him in our trials, rather whining, moaning, complaining and fretting all through them? Doesn't Scripture say, *"Fear not"* 365 times! I note for us to 'fear not' every day of our year!

My dearly beloved mom was a worrier. I remember thinking, I wonder if she feels that if she does not do her quota of worrying she is not doing her job as a mom? Can we relate? What better way to face the trials than to accept that God is on the throne, He is not about to leave, and that He wants us to be peaceful and not in turmoil.

I have heard people say, but you don't understand! What I understand is that as a Christian, I am required to believe the 'report of the Lord', and not that of man if I want to stay sane in these troubled times. I, too, have been disturbed by God many times, and I believe this was where the "rubber hit the road" for me as a believer. Was I always suc-cessful in placing my trials in His hand and being peaceful? No! However, as a "work in progress", I am very aware of my options, and counting on God's grace to bring me from Glory to Glory and get to a point where my feathers get ruffled less and less.

When Esther and her uncle accepted, embraced, and moved towards God as He brought them interruptions, a nation was saved. And Esther spent the rest of her days as queen, and much favored of God and man.

There is much turmoil in many of our lives, but He is there to calm the storms and say, *"Peace be still."* (Mark 4:39) Just like the time when a rough storm rocked all of them in a boat. It was Peter who sank when he took his eyes off of Jesus. (Matthew 8:23-27) We sink, too, when we take our eyes off of Him. I know I have experienced sinking like a rock. Why did I not remember He is "I Am", the God that never changes?

If God has done miracles in your lives, make a list and reflect on them when the ground under you starts shaking. And refresh your-self with another look at His promises in His Word, for they are faithful and sure.

Sometimes the uncertainties and trials from God we experience are intended to give us tes-timonies, or to help us to develop compassion, and/or passions for a future calling. As the eye of the storm is calm, so are you when you find Him. Scripture says, *"... we are the apple of His eye..."* (Psalm 17:8) We are protected by God. Through encounters with His presence you will find courage and peace, as Hagar did in Genesis 16:7-14. Frenzied activity just brings chaos. We are given many chances to become more and more like Him. His ways are so much for our benefit... if we could only get that into our hearts and spirits when the boats of our lives start rocking.

Something else that gives me peace is the scripture Romans 8:28. My perspective lately when something goes wrong is, "OK, Lord, I know you must have something better at hand." Though our vision tarries sometimes, He is faithful to deliver! Do you want to live your Christian walk on the cutting edge, the place where heaven and earth collide? I do!

Oswald Chambers says, "Lay it all before Him, and in the face of difficulty, bereavement and sorrow, hear Him say, *"Let not your heart be troubled."* (John 14:1) My Utmost for His Highest, August 26 Devotion (31)

Let's look up and reach for His Peace. It is there for the taking. It brings healing, restoration, and refreshment. That is where I want to be, I am sure you can all agree.

MEDITATION 23

Me, an Oak?

The Year of the LORD's Favor

"The Spirit of the Sovereign LORD is on me,
because the LORD has anointed me
to proclaim good news to the poor.
He has sent me to bind up the brokenhearted,
to proclaim freedom for the captives
and release from darkness for the prisoners,
to proclaim the year of the LORD's favor
and the day of vengeance of our God;
to comfort all who mourn,
and provide for those who grieve in Zion—
to bestow on them a crown of beauty
instead of ashes,
the oil of joy
instead of mourning,
and a garment of praise
instead of a spirit of despair.
They will be called oaks of righteousness,
a planting of the LORD
for the display of his splendor." (Isaiah 61:1-3)

This scripture happens to be my life scripture. I was imprinted with it just after I came to know Christ as my Lord and Savior, in 1979.

Back then, I lived in a small Cape Cod style home in Scottsville, NY. In the front yard were massive oak trees. I marveled at those great old giants and it was then that the Lord gave me Isaiah 61:1-3. My spirit lit up with this passage, especially verse 3, because it was a time in my life when I needed joy instead of mourning, and a garment of praise instead of my heaviness. I began to investigate oak trees.

I feel there are many significant reasons the Lord had selected oaks as a metaphor for righteousness, hence my focus today. Realize that we are not only talking about oaks, but also about being a *"planting of the Lord for the display of His splendor."* (Isaiah 61:3)

I think that is a loaded statement and full of promise from Him. This is not only for us, but as these three verses signified for me, a mandate from Him to not only for us to be the oak, but to raise up other oaks.

Let's talk about some qualities of oaks. The mighty oak is a symbol of courage and power and permanence. In the natural, legends suggest that it is the most powerful of all trees, the 'Mighty Oak' stands strong though all things. A tree in general is a symbol of antiquity and immense and enduring strength. Another general interpretation for a tree can be protection. Its body is rooted in the earth; oak tree roots spread wide and deep, while its crown dances in the sky. Other trees are symbolic of nurturing, as they bear fruit, and also of Eternal Life, as in Genesis 2:9, where we are introduced to Tree of Life.

Oaks bear fruit for smaller animals and house them as well; and when cut down, it is a very hard wood, valuable in building and making furniture, or in building homes or bridges. So, it is purposeful dead or alive! An oak's life span can be 500 to 1000 years. An oak will produce its first seed crop at 50-60 years. A single oak can produce upwards of 50,000 acorns.

Jesus (Yeshua) quoted parts of Isaiah's passage in his hometown synagogue (Luke 4:16-21) to describe His ministry to His people, and thus ours today. In it, God could have used any number of symbols to describe His plans to mature His people, but He chose to use a tree. In Scripture the Holy Spirit employs many trees to teach people His lessons. These apply to us, as you recall, because we Gentiles are grafted in to Christ, the King of Israel, who likens Himself to a vine.

Our inheritance is to be an Oak of Righteousness- a planting of the Lord. When the Lord plants something it is a permanent work. Scripture says that '...for God's gifts are irrevocable." (Romans 11:29) He is not going to change his mind; *"I the LORD do not change. So you, the descendants of Jacob, are not destroyed."* (Malachi 3:6.)

Where are we in our tree life? As believers this destiny is not only something we should aspire to, but also propagate in others, and so fulfilling scripture. I believe as we move to liberate others and deal with the trials in our lives, He will make us stronger and more flexible. As we ingest His Words, bask in His presence and worship and praise Him, these spiritual nutrients strengthen and nourish our root system. We grow stronger and taller in Him, yet our branches are free to wave in the wind. We can better minister to others and be that "City on a Hill" (Matthew 5:14) that all can see and come for refuge.

We produce fruit that becomes nourishment to others. We can provide shade and a resting spot for the weary to sit under. Yet our stature and strength stand above the rest! The older or more mature in Christ we become, the more crops we bear in Him; and knowing He has planted us, guarantee us eternal life. Are you mature in the Lord? You are not just getting older: you are getting ready to bear fruit. The tree was the venue of our salvation at Calvary!

These are just some thoughts I have been pondering for a long time and wanted to share. There are many 'Oaks' in the Word. If you are wondering what God is calling you to be, please examine the above scripture and what follows. It also goes on to say that He anointed us (empowered) to do these things in His Name and for His splendor. So if you think you are not qualified, remember, God does not call the qualified, He qualifies the called. Also remember that all Oaks start out as little acorns, but He protects them in their seedling stage and then brings them along to completeness. All we have to do is say yes, and He does the rest. I want to be an Oak, what about you?

MEDITATION 24

God's Tears

Yesterday I ventured out for my daily prayer walk, in a fine mist rain. At the end of that walk, I heard in my spirit, these are God's tears. I sensed that the waters you see, and the volume of rains covering many places these days, are indicative of the sorrow God is experiencing over our land, over the world. I sensed strongly God is weeping and grieving over the violence, lawlessness, immorality, Godlessness and compromise in the world today. Remember even *"Jesus wept."* (John 11:35)

I got the sense He was particularly sad over the condition of HIS BODY, on the earth. I found myself wondering at this point if he had reached the level of sorrow that he had after man fell, and darkness and debauchery had covered the earth, in the days of Noah. God pronounced that He was sorry that he had made man. (Genesis 6:6)

I felt sad that with all God had done , and has done it seems like we as a people have been caught up in the horizontal, and lost our Kingdom mentality, that truly we are sojourners on this planet, and have become worshippers and lovers of things, money, themselves and not of other people.

I found myself asking God for forgiveness for not only areas in my life that have disappointed Him, but on behalf of the human race at large, and for making Him weep. I got the sense that seeing those that call themselves His, and we not walking in truth and light, were the major source of His tears.

What does one do when they see one crying? You want to wipe away their tears. We need to be light in this dark world, and experience His joy, and be a joy to Him in every area of our lives.

Lord let us take seriously your heart, and seek you, and repent from our wicked ways, and live solely and wholly for YOU. Let us return to our first love...YOU. Let obedience be our hallmark, and bring Holiness back as the standard. Father, we are sorry and want to wipe your tears away, with lives that represent truly who you are. More of You Lord and less of us Father. Bring YOUR church back to its roots, and unify like never before. Let Your light shine in us, and when we are seen, what is visible to this world, is You!

> *"... weeping may endure a night, But joy comes in the morning. "* (Psalm 30:5 NKJV)

Let us be YOUR morning joy.

We want to be Sons that shine for You. Amen.

MEDITATION 25

Where the rubber hits the road

Recently I have been troubled by the war between my Kingdom thinking, and my actual circumstances. Have you ever been there? This is a post on FaceBook that Pastor Joshua Finley of Elim Gospel Church posted yesterday, "The Limitation Lie is that what you START with... you are STUCK with." Did that ever hit me in the face!

This is where our worldly belief system and the supernatural Resurrection Power of Jesus Christ collide, the dividing line between the TRUTH, and the world's truth and lies. Isn't that what is driving terrorist groups, Lies?!!! Are we really any different with some of our skewed thinking? Are our behaviors motivated by lack of knowledge, and assumptions? You cannot know the lies if you do not know the truth. Scripture speaks of those of God's elect that will be deceived in Mark 13:22.

Many churches are redefining the Bible according to modernist thinking. Scripture also says, "Woe to them that call evil good and good evil." (Isaiah 5:20)

Many churches and Christians also do not believe in the Resurrection Power of Jesus Christ, for this day. Talk about the miraculous is for a past day, not ours.

We are also being caught up in lies that keep us bound to the 'natural'; the enemy has cut many off at the knees, by dismantling the authority we have in Jesus Christ, and by diminishing the promise of greater things than these we will do in this day, and moving in this direction. We have become a LIMP and POWERLESS church. Is that not what the enemy wants? A limp and powerless church! The enemy is an opportunist and the enemy of our soul. He has the rest of the world his sights are on. Misery wants company!

When you look right at the circumstances in today's world, one could easily feel STUCK! If our thinking is STUCK, then we are STUCK. If our words are STUCK, then we will become STUCK. Being STUCK leads to fear and hopelessness, and it is all downhill from there! STUCK brings us to death and a standstill.

Sometimes GOD calls us out into the deep! Sometimes HE calls us to take steps that may look irrational according to our actual reality or world standards.

Jesus was our ultimate FORERUNNER in this area. He loved to upset the apple cart with miracles, signs and wonders! Not to mention turn the tables on the religious. He is what I would call a 'pot stirrer'. I believe HE is looking for pot stirrers in us.

Our actions take root in our thinking. We need to interrupt, and dismantle the lies, when they start in out in our heads, so we can move freely into the realm of the unknown, (faith). When we do this we will the supernatural, in our own lives and in the world! They say in a relationship if even one person changes the other will as well. We need to be world changers, and it starts one by one. But if we are STUCK, we can change nothing.

If GOD can raise Jesus Christ from the dead, HE can put a pot roast on our tables, and money in bank accounts, and so on.

If we don't embrace what HE has already given us, why do we bother at all, with our religious acts?

If we believe Jesus is the TRUTH, He is the model.

I was caught up with *my stuck*. My Bible says in Luke 1:37 that, *"For nothing is impossible with God."* What does yours say?

What is your STUCK today? It starts with dismantling the lies of what we can't do, with the truth of what we can do, and what we have been mandated to do by Jesus Himself.

Today the events in my life can look STUCK, but when I know the TRUTH which is Jesus, my faith is activated, and been rejuvenated the possibilities are limitless.

Just remember what Smith Wigglesworth did, when faced with the devil, ' "oh it's just you "and went back to his business of raising the dead in Jesus' Name.

Not even ISIS (32) can compare to what we can do when we move out of the realm of STUCK, into KINGDOM AUTHORITY and RESURRECTION POWER!

Ever wonder why third world countries see more of the miraculous, than us? Their only option is Jesus. They can't even take matters into their own hands to fix their STUCK. It is at the point of relinquishing their own under-standing, and abilities, and in blind faith- desperate for miracles, that they become Kingdom THINKERS, and are recipients of KINGDOM treasures and miracles. But in our highly developed country we say we can do it on our own, or we think GOD needs us to solve our problems, leaning on our own understanding and power. It is no wonder why nothing happens! It must sound like to GOD that we don't need Him!

I seriously think God is bringing us all to our knees, back to that childlike dependence on Him, with some of what is happening in the world today.

Sure, God gave me intelligence, but I am going to surrender that back to Him, for HIS

GLORY. He certainly knows me better than I do...He made me!

Sounds like the recipe is there to release answers to our many petitions, including the release of heart-stopping miracles, that will make the Bible come alive **in** us! In order to know the lies, you have to know the truth, and believe it. The truth is in HIS Word. This is where the rubber hits the road for me, what about you? IT'S ALL ABOUT HIM! Step up to the plate and HE will knock it out of the park!

MEDITATION 26

Changed from the Inside Out

In the process of writing this, I have covered a number of topics; although I felt led of the Lord to share primarily from the book of Esther. She was a great woman of God who came from humble beginnings but who found herself in the right place at the right time with reference to God's sovereign plans to save her people.

We have examined tools for effective intercession; the favor and authority that God has given us; what kinds of things God can do through us; and our positioning in life by God that may bring us favor and platform. We also looked at those positions when they feel uncomfortable because they may rest on a legal right (such being elected to office) which places us as God's woman or man on the job.

We talked about some of the things that may cause our spiritual demise; about our available keys to the Kingdom for breakthrough, healing, and resurrection power. We have previewed tasty delights that God offers us on His menu! We have also been encouraged with knowing that joy does come in the morning, and we have whet our appetites to become game-changers and do great exploits for Him.

I have shared a perspective showing that when we are 'disturbed', or our boats get rocked, it isn't always from the devil, but may be God Himself shaking our comfort levels in order to direct us. God sometimes leads with closed doors. We have learned about God's purpose to mature us into stately "oaks of righteousness" for His Kingdom Glory.

We are I believe, living in times where we are literally perched on the edge of Glory-His Glory. Especially in these difficult times awaiting His return. However, before that happens I believe we will experience the most Glory this earth has ever experienced to date. Why, because scripture tells us how Jesus demonstrated saving *'the best wine for last'* (Paraphrased-John 2:10) as He did in his first miracle at the wedding feast of Cana. I believe He is keeping the best "wine" ever for us in these end times! I am also hoping that for you, these meditations have been an exercise in being transformed, changed from the inside out, from Glory to Glory.

Lastly, we discussed the STUCK mentality.

It may look like to some that the sobering things going on in our government and world are beyond change, and that we are STUCK with what we have, or that we should just pray for an early rapture.

The truth is that we all need to do our part, and I believe it starts with 2 Chronicles 7:14, *"... if My people called by My Name, will humble themselves and pray and seek My face, and turn from their wicked ways, then I will hear from heaven, I WILL forgive their sins, and heal their land."* (NKJV)

We are not stuck, but we need to realize that the hope rests with us first (His body on this earth) to do our due diligence in seeking Him, and removing compromise, and rebellion out of our lives. We need self examination, prayer, and most importantly, we need repentance. It is the way! 1 John 3:8 tells us the Son of God appeared to destroy the devil's work. He is going to use us to do that. We can no longer look the other way, waiting for someone to do it for us. He will hold us accountable for not doing our part scripturally in the healing of our land. We can no longer say we did not know, and when we stand before Him, He may ask us, why did we not know? It is up to us to find out, and implement what we have learned. That being said, we can be used to change the world, one by one starting with number 1! Hosea 4:5 says, *"My people are destroyed from lack of knowledge."*

We know what the hope is and what the end of the story will be in scriptures; I heard it in my spirit on a prayer walk.

First, The Glory of Zion, from Isaiah 60.

"Arise, shine, for your light has come,
and the glory of the Lord rises upon you.
See, darkness covers the earth
and thick darkness is over the peoples,
but the Lord rises upon you
and his glory appears over you.
Nations will come to your light,
and kings to the brightness of your dawn.
Lift up your eyes and look about you:

All assemble and come to you;
your sons come from afar,
and your daughters are carried on the hip.
Then you will look and be radiant,
your heart will throb and swell with joy;
the wealth on the seas will be brought to you,
to you the riches of the nations will come.
Herds of camels will cover your land,
young camels of Midian and Ephah.
And all from Sheba will come,
bearing gold and incense
and proclaiming the praise of the Lord.
All Kedar's flocks will be gathered to you,
the rams of Nebaioth will serve you;
they will be accepted as offerings on my altar,
and I will adorn my glorious temple.

Who are these that fly along like clouds,
like doves to their nests?
Surely the islands look to me;

in the lead are the ships of Tarshish,
bringing your children from afar,
with their silver and gold,
to the honor of the Lord your God,
the Holy One of Israel,
for he has endowed you with splendor.
Foreigners will rebuild your walls,
and their kings will serve you.
Though in anger I struck you,
in favor I will show you compassion.
Your gates will always stand open,
they will never be shut, day or night,
so that people may bring you the wealth of the
nations—
their kings led in triumphal procession.
For the nation or kingdom that will not serve
you will perish;
it will be utterly ruined.

The glory of Lebanon will come to you,
the juniper, the fir and the cypress together,
to adorn my sanctuary;
and I will glorify the place for my feet.
The children of your oppressors will come
bowing before you;
all who despise you will bow down at your feet
and will call you the City of the Lord,
Zion of the Holy One of Israel.

Although you have been forsaken and hated,
with no one traveling through,

I will make you the everlasting pride
and the joy of all generations.
You will drink the milk of nations
and be nursed at royal breasts.
Then you will know that I, the LORD, am
your Savior,
your Redeemer, the Mighty One of Jacob.
Instead of bronze I will bring you gold,
and silver in place of iron.
Instead of wood I will bring you bronze,
and iron in place of stones.
I will make peace your governor
and well-being your ruler.
No longer will violence be heard in your land,
nor ruin or destruction within your borders,
but you will call your walls Salvation
and your gates Praise.
The sun will no more be your light by day,
nor will the brightness of the moon shine on you,
for the LORD will be your everlasting light,
and your God will be your glory.
Your sun will never set again,
and your moon will wane no more;
the LORD will be your everlasting light,
and your days of sorrow will end.
Then all your people will be righteous
and they will possess the land forever.
They are the shoot I have planted,
the work of my hands,
for the display of my splendor.
of you will become a thousand,

the smallest a mighty nation.
I am the Lord;
in its time I will do this swiftly."

The second scripture is from Song of Solomon 2: 9-10.

> *"My beloved is like a gazelle or a young stag. Behold, he stands behind our wall..."* (NKJV) Our beloved Jesus in calling to us!

Let us always keep our eternal perspective that we are sojourners here, and that every one of us has been given a plan and destiny, and that we are indeed marked by God's signet ring! He is looking through the windows; He is peering through the lattice.

> *"My beloved spoke and said to me, Arise, my darling, my beautiful one, come with me. See! The winter is past; the rains are over and gone."*
> (Song of Solomon 2:10-11)

Our Bridegroom is standing at the door offering for us hope now. His Kingdom is here and these verses light up my spirit to pray:

Father, I am so glad that we are here for such a time as this; that we can make a difference for You, before we go on to the next leg of our journey.

Thank you for twice choosing us. Help us to make the most of what we learn and to do your bidding.

Thank you God as you prepare us, as you did Esther , for our meeting with You, Oh King, and that we can see your scepter extended to us, and hear You say: 'What is it Queen Esther, Even up to half of the kingdom, it will be given unto you", (and heal our land).

Direct our steps, educate us, show us our part, bless us with courage and boldness, to spread the truth to all that need to hear it.

Bless each and every reader, and thank You for meeting our every need.

As we take care of Your people, we thank You that You take care of us.

Lord, we don't want to miss a heartbeat of what You have for us.

Keep us in Your Will.

Help us Lord, to look through the windshields or our lives and not the rear view mirrors, so we can lay hold of the now and forever.

Bless our land again, and return it to the Christian principles it was founded on!

In Your Name we pray. AMEN!

Post Script...

As we are changed internally we can become the world changers for SUCH A TIME AS THIS, as Esther was, and save our nation, now!

Epilogue:

He is saving the best wine for last!

Over the last week, I have ministered to two people who are wondering why God has not acted on their behalf, and wondering why others in their lives are seeing the LORD move His hands on their behalf, and where is He in their situation.

I heard questions and statements like,' I must be doing something wrong, God is mad at me, He does not love me", and so on.

I began praying about this with the first person, and found myself asking the LORD the same question myself. Why so long Lord? What I heard was to tell the first person," the LORD would have you re-read the story of the wedding feast at Cana,(John 2: 1-11), and that He wants me to tell you, He is saving the best wine for last, He is saving it for us!

Fast forward a couple of days, and I found myself saying the same thing to another person, who was vigorously shaking her head in agreement, that this indeed was her scenario too. I was able to lay hands on her, and instantly the anointing fell on her, not only for new wine, but the new wineskin to contain it! Please note, that before that moment, she spent some time openly repenting and renouncing unbelief, and some other issues that was putting static on her spiritual line.

I began to pray about this even further and the LORD, said to me, 'tell My people that even though I seem to be absent, and you wonder where I AM, tell them,

I AM:
I AM, Jehovah Nissi, My banner over them is love-Exodus 17:5
I AM, Jehovah Jireh, the GOD that provides-Genesis 22:14
I AM, El Shaddai, the Mighty Breasted One-Genesis 17:1
I AM, Jehovah Rapha, the LORD that heals-Exodus 15:26
I AM, Jehovah Sabaoth, the LORD of Hosts-Psalm 24:9-10
I AM, Jehovah Shammah, the LORD is there!-Ezekiel 48:35
I AM, Jehovah – Raah, the LORD My Shepherd-Psalm 23:1
I AM, El Olam, the Everlasting God'-Genesis 21:33

He went on to say tell my people, *"...I the LORD do not change..."* (Malachi 3:6)

> *'Therefore I will live up to My many Names. I have never left them, nor will I forsake them. When they see Me, they will find me'.*
>
> *'I am stretching My people for these end times, to walk in faith and not sight. I am stretching them to know My voice, in the absence of My word. Times are coming when you need to know who I AM, the truth of what I will do for them, and My nature, so they can stand in the midst of many voices. Tell them this is boot camp for the end time challenges'. "I am the GOD that is in the 'void and silent' times in their lives'.*

He also impressed on me that many times in the Bible, including the Wedding Feast at Cana, that HE waits until what feels to us, is the end of ourselves, when we are totally spent, and empty, to glorify Himself! Are you are in that position? Take heed you are pregnant for a movement of GOD. Please note that the wine did not show up, until there was no more left. Feeling empty and alone? You are poised for GLORY.

PROPHETIC MEDITATIONS ON ESTHER

Also imagine that the folks at the feast at Cana were possibly inebriated, and may not have even noticed the better quality wine. Folks when He shows up with the New Wine, let us not miss the moment, because we have been drunk on the world, complacent, or wining in our situations, or in our sin. Give Him praise in all things, relief is on the way! Be ready to drink it all in.

In that parable Jesus challenged His mother that it was not His time, but she proved Him, and went to the servants to prepare the water for the wine. The WORD says we have not, because we ask not. (Paraphrased James 4:21 and John 3:22) We also we need to believe that what we ask for in Him, we will receive.

Some of the responses I heard from those two individuals indicate to me that there is brokenness in that person, especially, unworthiness and abandonment issues, even anger, un-forgiveness, and bitterness.

By the way, remember also to forgive yourself. See yourself with the same blood-stained glasses, that Jesus sees us. In ourselves we are unrighteous, but when we come to Jesus, via the HOLY SPIRIT, HE makes us righteous. It is not a magic formula, but part of our inheritance. It takes work in our minds, to bring to captivity, those thoughts. For instance, when the evil one reminds us of our pasts, or sins, or tries to tell us that God has forsaken us, or when we are hit with condemnation, we need to recognize from when this comes from and refuse to entertain the lies.

Another issue is abandonment, especially for those that have experienced this from a biological parent. The natural inclination is to assume God will behave in a similar fashion. But HE is the one that states, *'we are children of GOD'*, and that will never change, and He is not like any earthly parent. (Paraphrased Roman 8:15)

In order to recognize the lies, we have to know the truth. The Bible also tells us that, *"Many are the afflictions of the righteous, But the LORD delivers him out of them all."* (Psalm 34:19 NKJV) So when the trials come, and they will, we already know the outcome, just not the timing!

Again, back to that feast at Cana, I am sure, even though it is not stated; the water was brought to Jesus in a fresh barrel, a clean one, before being changed into new wine. When wine ferments it expands and the container needs to be pliable enough so it does not burst. God is refashioning us in a way; I believe that will accommodate this new wine.

God is bringing us fresh wine skins, to pour out His new wine, into us for the greatest movement of God ever to be on this earth. Taking off the old skin can be painful, such as with debridement in a burn victim. But the new skin is fresh, and young and glowing, and pliable! This is not easy process.

He has many on track a forerunner remnant, to receive this New WINE, and the preparation process, is painful, as I said. Pain and trial, and duration of trial, does not mean rejection. We have a choice- embrace the process, and allow the old skins to come off in preparation for the new wine, or go where our comfort would have us go, the safe place, and miss what He has for us.

As Mary ignored Jesus' comment about not being His time to perform miracles, we can grab unto the horns of the altar and call down our miracles, and prove Him, like Elijah called down fire from heaven, that consumed all the water-everything. I am sure he really did not know for sure, what was going to happen, but it was not going to stop him from doing it. When we reach up to GOD, in such faith and desperation, He is there, to meet us at our point of need.

We need to be desperate, knowing that He is the only one that can fix our hurts. I believe that kind of faith is a sweet fragrance to Him, and even in weakness, if we can only offer up a feeble, 'help Jesus, He is there to truly be our Deliverer.

In all of this the LORD wants everyone to know, He has not forgotten us, and that His best wine is coming, and to prepare ourselves to receive what He has for us. The trials are the preparation and removal of old wineskins when we embrace the process, and sometimes the pain; and but for the Glory set before Him and us, it is coming and sooner than later. Indeed '

We are the Body of Christ, the embodiment of Him on this earth, and with all the authority that goes with that. *"Very truly I tell you, whoever believes in me will do the works I have been doing, and they will do even greater things than these, because I am going to the Father. And I will do whatever you ask in my name, so that the Father may be glorified in the Son. You may ask me for anything in my name, and I will do it."* (John 14:12-14)

Embrace the process. Know I AM is not going anywhere. He IS everywhere and, He is amongst us at <u>all times</u>!

Believe and receive!

The BEST WINE IS COMING, and last is NOT least!

Rev Jo

References And Footnotes

(1) Facebook© – an online social networking service. Website was launched on February 04, 2004 by Mark Zuckerberg, Eduardo Saverin, Andrew McCollum, Dustin Moskovitz and Chris Hughes

(2) Pastors Mark and Deborah Griffo senior pastors of Glory Mountain Church

(2a) Glory Mountain Church is located in San Marcos, California, www.glorymountain.com

(3) Pastors Brad and Carolyn Kuechler are senior pastors of Rock Solid Revival Center located in San Pedro, CA.

(3a) Rock Solid Revival Center, a church located in San Pedro, California, www.rocksolidsanpedro.org

(4) Samaritan Walks is a ministry dedicated to supply shoes for the needy worldwide. www.swalks.org

(5) Pastor Josh Finley is the lead pastor of Elim Gospel Church

(5a) Pastor Eric Scott, is the Care & Missions Director for Elim Gospel Church

(5b) Elim Gospel Church is located in Lima, NY, www. elimgospel.org

(6) Pastors Rene and Amber Picota, senior pastors at Streams of Life Church

(6a) Streams of Life Church is located in in Winchester, VA in the Aloft Hotel®

(6b) Aloft Winchester Hotel® is located in Winchester, VA and is a property of the Starwood Hotels & Resort®, worldwide

(7) Julie Price is the author/writer/blogger on Spirit Fuel©

(7a) Spirit Fuel© is a Facebook© page devotional and Website (wwww.spiritfuel.me, managing members: Joel Yount and Thomas Griffin) for Christians

(8) Merriam-Webster's Dictionary, Inc. ©/online- ("Webster's Dictionary©–1864- the inventors of the modern dictionary")

(9) Bill & Marsha Burns are senior pastors at Faith Tabernacle in Kremmling, CO. They are also the writers of the Facebook© devotional and website of "Small Straws in a Soft Wind (www.ft111.com)

(10) Bill Yount is a Christian evangelist who travels the world bringing God's Word to those who need to hear it. He is the founder of "Blowing the Shofar Ministries©" www.Billyount.com

(11) Strong's Concordance© (also known as The Exhaustive Concordance of the Bible©- is Bible study resource guide; originally constructed by Dr. James Strong 1822-1894, printed in New York by Eaton & Mann©, Cincinnati by Jennings & Graham©-1890),

(12) Jell-O™ is the registered trademark of Kraft Foods™, a gelatin dessert.

(13) Oswald Chambers (1874-1917) was a Scottish evangelist and teacher.

(14) My Utmost for His Highest©–Oswald Chambers-a Christian daily devotional first published in 1935 and is currently under the Discovery House Publishers-Grand Rapids, MI (excerpt- June 20th)

(15) New Age–a religious or spiritual movement that was in the late 1600's, but was recognized in the 1970's.; compiled but not limited to a variety of Asian religions, meta-physics and psychology to name a few. Two nineteenth philosophers-Helena Blavatsky(1831-1891) and G.I. Gurdjieff (1872-1949) greatly influenced this modern movement.

(16) Reinhard Bonnke (1940-) is a German evangelist, known to concentrate primarily in Africa.

(17) My Utmost for His Highest© by Oswald Chambers-(excerpt from July 18)

(18) Aimee Semple McPherson (1890-1944)–also known as "Sister Aimee", was a Canadian-American Christian evangelist in the 1920-30's.

(19) The International Church of the Foursquare Gospel–also known as the Foursquare Church is a protestant Christian denomination founded in 1923 by the late Aimee Semple McPherson. www.foursquare.org

(20) Kathryn J. Kuhlman (1907-1976) was an American Christian evangelist,

(21) Maria Woodworth-Etter (1844-1924)–was an American Christian healing evangelist.

(22) Smith Wigglesworth (1859-1947) was a British evangelist and faith healer.

(23) Break Every Chain©–authors- Jeffery S. Ferguson, Regi Stone, Belden Street Music Publishing

(24) Facing the Giants©–2006 American Christian drama, directed by Alex Kendrick, volunteer cast from Sherwood Baptist Church (Albany, GA), Sherwood Pictures, Samuel Goldwyn Films

(25) Billy Graham (1918-) is an American Christian evangelist, www billygraham.org

(26) President John F. Kennedy (1917-1963) was the 35th American president of the United States of America

(27) Excerpt from President Kennedy's inaugural address–the final lines.

(28) Hannah Hurnard (1905-1990) was a Chinese-English Christian author.

(29) Hind's Feet in High Places is an allegorical novel by Hannah Hurnard

(30) A Marine–a man or woman enlisted in the United States Marine Corp., a branch of the Armed Forces

(31) My Upmost for His Highest Devotional © by Oswald Chambers excerpt from August 26

(32) ISIS–or The Islamic State of Iraq is a Salafi jihadist extremist militant group of terrorists

About Josephine Ayers

Reverend Josephine (Jo) M. Ayers is a wife of 22 years; mother, grandmother and devout lover of GOD. She was ordained and licensed under Glory Mountain, International, San Marcos, CA. She attended Elim Bible Institute-Lima, NY.

Josephine's past accomplishments, include (but not limited to) RN, CA-RE/Notary,service in the So. California Women's Aglow Prison Ministry, the San Diego Women's Aglow Area Team, Worship Ministry, Deliverance Ministry, her own ministry, Setting the Captives Free, Elim Gospel Church- Prophetic and Healing and Release Teams, Small Groups leader.

Today, Josephine is moderating a closed Face book prayer page, called Esther's Intercessors, and ministering with Rochester New York Healing Rooms, EGC Influencer.

Her hobbies include, cooking, gardening, singing, writing, guitar playing, fishing, computering, and blogging.

1458 Rochester St
B
LIMA NY
14485

951-237-2800

CPSIA information can be obtained at www.ICGtesting.com
Printed in the USA
BVOW02s0050061115

425933BV00001B/4/P

9 781498 452083